COLLECTED POEMS

Also by Susan Noble

Before and After the Darkness
The Dream of Stairs: A Poem Cycle
Drifting Between Empty Tramlines
A Flock of Blackbirds
Inside the Stretch of My Heart

COLLECTED POEMS

The Dream of Stairs: A Poem Cycle

Inside the Stretch of My Heart

Before and After the Darkness

Susan Noble

AESOP Poets
Oxford

AESOP Poets
An imprint of AESOP Publications
Martin Noble Editorial / AESOP
28 Abberbury Road, Oxford OX4 4ES, UK
www.aesopbooks.com

First paperback edition published by AESOP Publications

First edition of *The Dream of Stairs*
printed privately in 1975.

The Dream of Stairs, 2nd edition,
Inside the Stretch of My Heart and
Before and After the Darkness
published in separate editions
by AESOP Publications, 2014.

ISBN: 978-1-910301-09-8

CONTENTS

CONTENTS

CONTENTS

CONTENTS

CONTENTS

PART VII   THE NINGO PIN   **187**

CONTENTS

CONTENTS

PART IV EVENING

PART V NIGHT   **357**

PART VI INDOORS   **371**

CONTENTS

CONTENTS

3 BEFORE AND AFTER THE DARKNESS 459

Preface

About the book

Collected Poems by Susan Noble incorporates three collections of poems: *The Dream of Stairs: A Poem Cycle*; *Inside the Stretch of My Heart*; and *Before and After the Darkness*. To mark the fortieth anniversary of her death, this comprehensive volume is being published in hardback, paperback and Kindle, making all her poems publicly available for the first time.

The Dream of Stairs was privately printed as a posthumous memorial volume in 1975, a year after my sister Susan's untimely death in 1974 at the age of 31. Having announced with typically light-hearted self-depreciation that 'The muse has struck me!', Susan wrote the poems in batches of half a dozen or more from 1965 onwards in what she described as manic bursts of creativity. But these poems are anything but light-hearted, and even a first reading will reveal clearly that levity is not on the menu in a universe 'Where there are no jokes / And people do not pretend.'

Susan's output in the last ten years of her life was prolific, but when it came to compiling the poems, after a good deal of deliberation, a clear thematic structure and underlying development seemed to dictate the final order of that original poignant collection.

There are a number of changes to the first edition: a slight reordering of the poems, minor amendments to the structure of the poem cycle, a revised, enhanced layout, and indexes of titles and first lines. More significantly, the original selection has been augmented by many additional poems, which clearly fit within the cycle thematically and structurally.

Many of the poems in *Inside the Stretch of My Heart* were triggered by the quotidian experience of living and working in central London in the late 1960s and early 1970s, yet beneath the fragile surface of her acute observations of domestic and office life in the city, intensely spiritual insights are being played out, sometimes delicately, sometimes shockingly, but always movingly.

The poems in the third collection in this volume, *Before and After the Darkness*, were written in the early 1970s, like those in *Inside the Stretch of My Heart*, and include a number of poems written in 1973 and 1974 in the months before Susan's death.

Two further companion volumes are also being published: *A Flock of Blackbirds* (selected novellas and short stories); and her novel, *Drifting Between Empty Tramlines*.

Profits from the sales of all six volumes are being donated to three charities: Mind, the Samaritans and Sane. For more details, see page xxiv.

Facsimiles of the original typescripts and manuscripts are available online at:

www.aesopbooks.com/susannoble

Martin Noble
Oxford, 2014

About the author

Brought up in South London, my sister, Susan Noble, was the second of three children. Her childhood was enriched by being part of our large and closely-knit Jewish family. Unfortunately stricken by polio (then known as infantile paralysis) in her early years, Susan went through life with a degree of physical handicap which she was to overcome with courage and determination.

Educated at Croydon High School, Susan studied English at Somerville College, Oxford. After graduating, Susan worked in London, first at the Royal National Institute for the Blind, dictating books for transcription into Braille, and later at the National Central Library in London, where she qualified as a Chartered Librarian.

Susan's exceptional sensitivity was reflected in the prolific out-pouring of poems to be found in *The Dream of Stairs, Inside the Stretch of My Heart* and *Before and After the Darkness*. In these intense, haunting poems, she chronicles her personal response to the world around her, while vividly portraying the inner landscape of her mental and emotional struggle.

Judith Frankel
Netanya, 2014

Susan Noble

One's first impression of Susan was of fragility. She was an acutely sensitive person, but her physical and emotional fragility really masked a very great spiritual strength.

Her sensitivity indeed was not directed only towards herself, but towards others. She was sensitive to the needs of others, and her strength and also perhaps some of her inner conflicts came from a deep desire for goodness which could not be matched in reality by the world as she found it.

Susan passionately wished to be independent; she struggled for it from the time she went to university, and throughout her work as a librarian, and she was able to maintain it to the very end.

There was an intellectual and emotional intensity which burned within her and which predominantly found outward expression in her writing and when she expressed herself thus she did so with great imaginative power and also with an uncompromising honesty and integrity.

The late Rabbi Dr David Goldstein
South London, July 1974

Publisher's note

All profits from the sale of this volume
are being donated to the following charities:

The National Association for Mental Health
www.mind.org.uk

SAMARITANS

www.samaritans.org

SANE

www.sane.org.uk

THE DREAM OF STAIRS

Prologue: To Create

A poem cannot be contrived wilfully,
But grows out of a black knot;
The sharp needle unravels the tangled lump
Into a long thread of the imagination,
Which can be cut into shreds
Or resolved into a tight knot once again.

PART I

THE HARD ROAD

1   *The Hard Road*

You have chosen the hard road,
The hard road and the steep hill,
Where there are no jokes
And people do not pretend.

You have chosen the stretching rack,
Where there is no sofa to sink into,
No easy way out,
And no crutch of creed to rest upon.

You see the daylight,
White and sometimes silvery,
But most of the time grey, greylight,
You have chosen the hard road.

2 Apple-Blossom Scent

Apple-blossom scent,
Sickly strong,
Sends me hurtling through the tunnel of time
To a class in a college common-room ten years ago.
Long wooden table, unvarnished, raw.
Twelve girls, mushroom faces, straight hair,
Cold on a summer's day.
Green quadrangle through the window,
Dons drifting past
In twos and threes
After a meeting.
Locked in a bottle of air, apple-blossom scent,
I cannot understand the silent thinking of the faces
Motionless around the table.
Contemptuous, I want to escape into the sunlight.
But now that the years have passed a new decade,
I find that these girls have run away
In different directions,
And I am still seeking too late to recapture
The thinking, which I forgot to do
In my adolescence.

3 Quick Birth

Reality painful
As gasping fish out of water
Breathes
Fills its lungs
Crying
Shapes
Of colour and sound and blurred
Movements
From warmth of waters
Into sharp-edged air

4   Life Story

Born to a bellow of music outside the hospital window,
The nurse consoled my mother, 'It's only a sousaphone.'
My mother was soothed, but I was not.
And as the years passed by,
I roared in anger at every passing image.
Slowly the music turned into waves of acceptance,
Crotchet upon quaver, staccato surprise.
And now I wait in silence for the next chord.

5   *Nice Child*

When I was a child, a naughty child,
I watched the nice little girl play with her hair-ribbon.
She wore a lemon and white gingham dress
Of glazed cotton,
And her plaits were looped into glazed yellow bows.
Her forehead was large and serene
As she sat on the carpet quietly thinking.
When I was a child, I wanted to be that nice little girl,
And now against my will, it seems,
I have changed into what she was,
And when a thought passes through my mind
I filter it with pursed lips.
Is this a change for the better
Or do I no longer exist?

6   Cousins

Cousins
Are siblings once removed and hover between
The fence of friendship
And the telepathic silence of blood-bondage,
Puppet figures, that assert their distance,
And fall back in a quick glance
To the common patterns two generations ago.
An echoed laugh, twin chortles will surprise
In the face of alien accents, opposite gestures.
Only the curve of the thumb against the palm
Reminds us that we are falling away from the old stencil
And our children's children will stare at each other
Like strangers.

7 *Preview*

The first time I glimpsed Hell
Was on a Sunday afternoon,
Lounging on the red velveteen sofa.
The radio blared a gospel sermon,
That to neglect this message was black.
There was no turning back,
And the sofa changed to a sea of waves,
Tiny stinging ants probing the corrupted corpse,
Grey tongues of water lashing eternally.
The cat on the cushion by my feet purred
And washed her face
With the side of a grey paw,
The fur grown old from years of running up and down
In no particular direction,
Whichever way her energy disposed.
The yellow bow round her neck curved
In mock strangulation,
But she continued to purr a telephone buzz,
Reassuring in its regularity.
The first time I glimpsed Hell
Was only for a moment,
And afterwards I listened to the afternoon play
In front of the electric fire
And read the colour supplement in the glowlight,
Reassured by the artificial coals.

PART II

CHASTITY

8   *Chastity*

I am pale and white
Calm and quiet
Cool and bright.
What has never known never wants
And what has never wanted never needs.
I know there is a realm beyond my sphere
And what is unexperienced can lead to fear.
I fear and want not, want and fear not,
Know that I don't have and have what I don't know.
Day comes and is bright and light,
Night comes and is dark and black.
Day I know – night I know not.
Come hither – come not.
Cool and bright
Calm and quiet
I am pale and white.

9   *Grape Picking*

Slowly the sweet-sour juice trickling
From the spilled cluster
Is sucked up by the hot grass beneath the vines.
The sun is flat and hot on our covered heads.
The windowing vine-leaves protect
The heads of the grape bunches
Which peep out unaware of the midday heat.
The work is slow and rhythmic yet full of complications.
This bunch is second-grade so must be discarded.
The sabra-girl is fat and copper in the sunlight.
The grapes are sweet and bursting in the bushes.

10 *Midday*

Discovered
Sucking slowly on a straw
Gazing at the rosebush in the park,
Thinking of the colours, not of the bottle in my hand,
I blushed as he walked past,
Caught in the act
Remnant of babyhood.
He could never know the thought process,
Analysis of the trembling leaves
Curved downwards, rubbery oil-like surface,
Twitching greenery as the breeze flickers past,
Vulnerable to each vibration
Just as I am,
In his sight, a fool regressed
To slow sucking on a straw alone in a lunch-hour park.

11   *The Rendezvous*

His moccasins spattered with green mud of Chelsea,
Sardonically smiling with elegant sweetness
About to encounter the girl of his wanting,
Who is young and spry,
Graceful with eyelids enchanting.
The sand-dunes are sinking,
The sand-dunes are sinking,
Make love while you're young
And leave later your thinking.

They eat in a delicate Indian tea-place,
A well-chosen meal with some tentative chatter.
She's tongue-tied and pausing, but it does not matter,
The cigarette smoke counteracts the cool silence.
The sand-dunes are sinking,
The sand-dunes are sinking,
Make love while you're young
And leave later your thinking.

12 *First Love*

All that summer
The trees cracked into triangles,
The sunlight over the fences.
She waited for his letters.
Two lines were enough
For the words to dance like ants.
Along the streets people in silent cauls
Broke through into smiles.
The campus was littered with waving arms.
Fish in the sea,
Fluorescent,
Leaping silver,
Remember always.

13 *The Ballroom*

Lilting and loving, loving and lilting,
The music is playing, the flowers are wilting,
The ballroom is heated, the lightbulbs are fizzing,
I'm whirling and twirling, now spinning and dizzy.
Nothing is static, all's mobile and busy.
My partner's refilling the wineglass I'm tilting.
Lilting and loving, loving and lilting.
I'm dizzy, I'm spinning, my wine is o'erspilling,
The music is frisky and happy and trilling,
Willing us to dance and we are so willing.
Lilting and loving, loving and lilting.

14 *Falling*

The falling in love down through a hole in the heart
Through the bubbling blood, that bounces,
Day after day,
On a hope, that may come to nothing.
Daisy chain, will he, won't he?
White petals grow around the yellow pollen,
Will never stop curling,
Petal-points moist in the sunlight.
Can never stop loving.

15 Spellbound

This hypnotist
Has a sandalwood voice
That cracks in the middle and vibrates
Like layers of brown leather.
There is a blackness in his laugh,
In his prune eyes and beetle brows.
I am not afraid, simply magnetised.
The air around him hangs with violet dust,
Pulling me outwards, far away
To bluebells growing in a wood, prickly in the spring,
Beneath crackling branches
And then deep down, down
To the gloom of a hut in winter,
A light shining flat upon the ceiling,
Onto a body asleep.
There is pain here and some apprehension.
His voice crackles, buzzes into my ear,
The light is bright, two tiny specks in his eyes,
Now blue, now purple,
Glassy curve of iris.
The bluebells in the wood smell of sandalwood.
I want to stay here, here in this violet pool,
Drunk with submission,
Compelled to rest within the two tiny speckles
Gleaming from the very pit of his apprehension.

16 *Protection*

To be loved
Is to stop thinking.
Lampposts, restaurants, trees
Gaze back admiringly.
Barriers are crushed all around.
Skin pores stretch, take gulps of afternoon air,
Hair sways,
Nonchalance of the swinging breeze.

17   *When You Love Someone So Strangely*

When you love someone so strangely
That to stretch out through the air
Is to crack the tree-trunks into splintering thongs,
The ground is shattered into a thousand cracks
And the white sky falls down on top of your head,
A woolly weight from which there is no escape.
If you could reach him at this moment in time
And sink within the squeezing ventricles of his heart,
You would become his blood and bone.
There is no unity possible,
No way to evade the cut of pain as he walks
Away down the pavement,
A black figure ambling into the distance,
Out of sight and entering a new pattern of time
Beyond the blurred edge of your shadow.

18   *When His Arms Closed Around You*

When his arms closed around you,
Warm peace of dovelike knowing,
Rocking-chair haven of flesh,
You were cut off from the turbulence of life
With the rubber-edged knife;
And the morning after
Your fingernails scraped away
The numb dust of white palms
Into daylight.

Myopically I see him only at close range,
His thoughts, glances,
The grim thinking of his mouth, corners turned down.
Large eyes, black, anxiously they watch.
He fingers a yellow sideburn.
Envious, I hear the other discuss him as a person
In restaurants and theatres,
This dining-room, that party,
But I am trapped by my vision, almost a pointillism.
Grain upon grain I see, pore upon pore,
A magnifying glass to enlarge every gesture.
Which of us is right?

19   *Smile*

'Why do you smile all the time,' he asked,
'That stupid smile? What does it mean?'
'I see the discrepancy, the irony of things.'
'Stop observing and try to feel.
You have no feelings, no feelings of your own.'
He thumped his hand against his knee.
Black beard jerked against the corner of the mantelpiece
In the background.
'Yes, I do feel, but I observe as well,
And the difference between the two makes me laugh.'
She giggled, unable to stop, and swayed to and fro.
'Go on laughing,' he said. 'Laugh as much as you like.
Laugh and laugh and laugh.'
She laughed and laughed
And laughed and laughed again.
And then she felt that there was nothing left to laugh at,
So she stopped and sighed with the weight of loneliness.
He stared at her, satisfied.
And his face relaxed into a flicker of a ghost of a smile.
And they became acquainted with one another.

20   *The Couple*

You lay above me, cutting off the blue
Thick slice of sky that tried participation
In our secret individual conversation,
But I ignored the sky and wanted only you.

The time hung archetypal, slow and true,
For nations full have known the peace and pride,
When man and woman slumber side by side
Multitudes since and centuries ago.

The blue sky crumpled brown in jealous whim
And rain burst down upon us, pricking cold,
And purged us of our wisdom aeons old
And I was cold again, still loving him.

21   *The Killing*

He mocked her drawing,
Black criss-crossed edges of ink overlapping
To form a half-smile portrait.
He found the composition banal,
Which she had carefully fitted
Into the afternoon shade.
And when in recompense he admired
Her glow of rusty hair, long cheekbone,
She felt no pride, but changed unwittingly
Into a child, placated
Too late.

22 *Confession*

We sat in the damp evening air,
Soaking in the green grass.
The firm press of the park-bench.
Far out on all sides trees and white sky
And the cold vacuum of September
Stretching out, no barriers, no future.
At that moment, gust of wind
Against the mouldering ground,
We confessed our fear,
The fear of the surging crowds
And the things that cannot be understood,
The dwindling away of love and the sting
Of a wasp probing further and further,
And between us there grew a bond not of affection,
But the steel halter that straps two children together
As they freeze in their beds on a black November night
And listen to the monotonous creak of the rocking chair
As it shudders in the wind.

23 *The Quarrel*

They didn't mean to quarrel.
It just happened,
Crackling sun pressing down their hair,
Burning their necks, melting their fingers into dampness.
She disliked his accent.
His mistrusted her frivolity.
The quarrel cracked between them
Like a nut
And they were left to chew over the fragments,
Spitting out the splinters of woody shell,
That were lodged within it,
Blushing at their own coarseness,
Regressed to childhood
Squabbling.

24 *After the Quarrel*

After the quarrel
We sat in the night-blackened room
The curtains drawn open
Onto the rain outside.
It fell quickly in liquid pincers,
Slicing up the stones.
The branches trembled like spiders,
Grown old from years of steady rootage
And the clouds were drained green,
Exhausted by the downpour.
We sat and waited, as the furniture in the room
Grew white from the concrete yard outside,
Reflected through the blurred glass,
Whiteness like streaks of old salt.

25   *Parting*

If we never see each other again,
A sensible snipping away, which may perhaps happen
According to the slow blow of time
That has been dragging us down into a black quicksand,
Then I will be reconciled.
It will not be an easy chopping
Nor a simple conclusion to an old bond,
For here was no spell that held us down,
Except the quick sparring of minds at ease
Turbulent against the forces of life
That found sometimes a silent peace
Under the gold evening glow
When words had petered away
And had thrown us back
Into some past world long ago
Where we had been unified,
Black shadows downwards
Into the peace of the cave.
If we never see each other again,
Then I will be reconciled.
For some strange ebony wing brought us together
To lash one another with the fury of polarity
Until we merged into a surprised similarity
And now it is time for us to flow away again
Back into separation.

26 *Rejection*

I have wilfully flicked an ounce of flesh
Off his back with my Shylock knife.
I will not be dissuaded by drooping glances
Or the firm, door-blocking stance.
But leave straight away
With blinkered stare-ahead indifference
And wonder later why I feel no remorse
For a deed that was not unjust.

27   *The Laughter*

The laughter grew
Into gold coils.
It fizzled up the dark hours,
As fish grin in flashes
Around a weed
Deeply embedded
Within roots of mud and stone.
It eclipsed the sun,
That would have shone black
In the knowledge of what cannot be resolved,
As layer upon layer
Is peeled away
In the atomic dazzle at dawn.
The laughed clanged sombrely.
It re-echoed and burnt away the apprehensions,
That had bound us together
And we were soldered into one dead golden ring.

28 *Cut-outs*

When we met,
Cardboard figures
From a children's game,
I could not penetrate beneath
The quiet stance and watchful hostility;
And when six months later the surface was shattered,
I wanted to retrieve the wasted hours of polarity
And could not reach close enough,
As I clung on to those firm shoulders
Like a child soothed to sleep after a storm.

29   *Water-Bird*

Parabola of water.
Hoop bent together mischievously,
The left curve a smooth line of white,
And the right curve snipped off into droplets,
Bouncing against the water-coated concrete with a smash,
Painful spurts out in all directions
Into sharp water-spikes.
A hopping bird nearby nibbles the residue of water
With its beak,
Chewing the jumping lumps of white liquid,
Wings flutter, frantically
Shivering,
Longs to be rubbed dry, caressed into warmth,
But instead flaps around the concrete for two minutes
To raise the blood level,
So that it can hop under the dripping parabola again
And nibble lumps of water.

30   *Cotton-Wool Words*

Cotton-wool words,
Cloud-spun, cloud-spun,
A whirling white ball of candy-floss.
Words that do not echo you,
Words that do not echo me.
Let them consume themselves in cannibalism
And the air will speak between us.

31 *Separation*

Our love, fulfilled, would not be so.
Better to separate us between rows
Of houses, wall after wall,
Like a pack of trick cards,
Carefully assembled.
To join us would send the pack
Flying over into a heap.
Thinking of you,
I focus my attention upon a patch of wallpaper,
Cream and gold panels jutting out
From a white background,
Thick woolly paper,
If speared with a blade it would sag
And tear into a feathered edge,
The knife point lodged within the brittle plaster
Would scratch a shower of chalky crumbs,
The illusion of gold quietly explained.
Seldom we see each other from year,
Only a glimpse,
Your retreating figure down a side-street,
Face on a bus in profile, immobile in thought,
Through a buzz of conversation,
A flicker of laughter,
Echoes of a bond.
It survives eagerly,
Anticipating the impossible.

32   *Gift*

No security is possible, gateway to your love.
I cannot banish the fear of the door closed in my face
On a winter's afternoon at four o'clock ebb-tide,
Black gates iron-strong against the white sky.
No promises can ever give me
The golden sea of oblivion,
Anaesthetising the cut of the wind.
Only by your sudden whim,
When all the world is flattened to a concrete slab
And no thought-shadows flicker across my mind,
Do I glimpse the wave of love in your probing eyes.

33   *Clam*

You know I feel for you,
Your every motion.
Your look darts hatred at their empathy,
Which draws me beneath your skin
Into the marrow of your bones
To find strength in your hesitations.
I see your eyes blink black and narrow
Against the watchful grey of my glance.
I cannot detach it, snip it away,
Quick flip of elastic boomerang,
Only wish to remain a clam-parasite for ever.

34   *Chicken Bone*

I could tear you out of me,
Chicken bone swallowed and gone down the wrong way
To choke me continually;
And sometimes when the breath returns, I feel your love,
Eyes mobile, gazing hard,
And then the choking begins again.
I cannot decide whether the bone is an injury to my body
Or whether it is the spur
That keeps me gasping for more breath.

35 *Spiral of Light*

Knowing how he does not love you,
You fall through the side of a mountain,
Ribcage of rocks
Will open,
When all other ways are barred.
When Adam gave Eve his rib,
He grew unmanned, exultant.
In this there is no giving.
Now you wait for the darkness to trample,
Abate.
Leaving a spiral of light
White as shining eyes,
That beg you to accept
All imperfections.

36   Wandering Through the Days

Wandering through the days
With you lodged in my heart.
Explosion of living difference
Beaten into flesh.
I count the moments
Of no-clock time
Until the mirror will turn silver
With surprise.

37   *Passing*

Standing in the black rain
By the mud-wet bicycle,
Curve of steel glistening
Beneath the light of the shop-façade
I saw him approach,
Beanpole tall against the horizontal of the kerbside
And the flattened car-tops that zoomed by,
Lamp-post silhouette, that hovered against my own,
And willed me to speak.
Mud silence filled my mouth,
Clodded up my ears and stuffed my throat
With numb invisibility.
Slowly his shadow loped past,
Jutting upwards,
Leaving me diminished, squat,
Crunched flat as the car-tops that zoomed by.

38 *Burnt Out by the Shadows*

Our friendship came to nothing, petered away,
Not by a quarrel,
But burnt out by the shadows
Of the room, where we sat
And could not bridge the gap,
Because of your pride, my subservience.
It echoed in my mind, yawning over the years.
Now on a September evening,
Six o'clock in the flickering twilight,
We collide at the corner of a street.
The buzzing traffic, the click of passing shoppers
Roll away the differences between us,
And there is only a white stretch of pavement
And an airy smile.

39 *Facets*

Please believe
That I want nothing more from you,
Nothing at all,
And if you disbelieve this.
Then know, at least, that you
Are under no obligation to give it.
The years have plaited thread between us,
And trapped within our web other lives.
They have filtered away the things
That we believed in long ago
Before the age of complexity began.
Who can recognise the truth any more
Of a word, of a psalm, of an idea,
As layer upon layer is peeled away
With an awareness of reality so vivid
That it negates itself, having lost the conflict
Of surprised consciousness?
So I can only say to you again,
Please believe
That I want nothing more from you,
Nothing at all,
And if I did want it,
How would I know whether the wanting was a real wish,
Or a wanting of a wanting,
Or a wanting to be wanted?

40   *The Aim*

You can try
For a minute, for an hour, for a year,
To win his love, her love.
Stony defences thrown your efforts back
Jakari-like into your face,
And your features. blunted by denial,
Do not fit together any more.
Then on a sunny day in a crowd,
Unthinking, unwanting, uncalculating, you smile
As you step off the kerb,
And realise that a lifetime's exertions can come to nothing
And a face smiles back.
Whose face? It does not matter.
The dart has hit the bullseye by mistake.
It is not gratitude that you feel,
Only surprise,
Wry acceptance.

41   *Rope*

High above the earth
Upon a tightrope
A man and a woman
Step away the days
High and straight as the crow flies.
He will not hold her hand
Ruthless the gap between their wrists
Clenched to exertion
Far below the snow is flaked into layers of whiteness
Caught upon the mounds of the hillsides
And the sky is as black as a gleaming tin-can.
Silk
Of breath and snow and sky,
Silk of skin sinking into terror,
Ankle over ankle upon the rope.
There are no milestones,
No cuts to totem the pole,
To tell of the days
That remain to be stayed.
Some love there will be
Between the man and the woman
And the stepping over will go on,
Over and on.

42 *The Wedding*

Ten years ago they sat together at a wedding.
She smiled across the table, excluding him,
Smug and secure in her pink satin.
She nibbled prawns, a gleaming silver fork,
Plump arms waving, perfume and the band.
She laughed aloud. Confident she saw
Everything in black and white,
While he hovered foolishly in the background,
Hesitated,
Seeing the stripes, the grey.

And now he walks past her in the street,
Long strides, heedless.
And she hesitates, seeing the grains, the shadows.
But he has forgotten her completely,
A vacant doll,
And she must bear the double lash
Of total daylight
And his ignorance.

43 *Restoration*

Can it ever be recovered,
Integrity of childhood?
Bird nibbling cherry in the hay,
Wisps of yellow grass beneath the hot sun,
Restored to the old, old frozen self.
Snowflakes dripping down the silk of cheeks
On a January morning.
All is swept away by the brush of love,
Yellow flame burns away the dust
And leaves a new face,
Burnished with understanding.

44   *False Image*

Crossing the road,
I thought I recognised a familiar face,
A mistake,
Which caused the face to split in two,
The face of a stranger nonchalantly aloof
And the face of a friend in open communication,
And as we passed the island in the middle
It switched itself into a different key,
Aware that it had to fit an unknown pattern
And recognising itself from my surprise
Where I was aware of this imposition,
Erased from those features the old remembered shadows,
Leaving the scrubbed detachment of a stranger.

45   *Remember*

At the end of the long day,
When the leaves of the oak-trees rattle,
And sleepy officer-workers march home
In twos and threes,
I remember the sabra-boy with the guitar,
Blue shirt and spade of ginger beard,
Thick features stretched into a grin,
Rattle of whining music.
The scratch of cat gut, the blur of discords,
The cry of our ancestors in the ghettoes,
Before they left the pogroms for an alien way of life.
The leaves rattle
And the guitar slurs.
The roaring traffic blurs with the scream
Of generations ago,
Crying, dying in heaps,
A yellow scarf spotted with blood
And a pair of stiff leather shoes
Thrown down a flight of stairs
By an old woman in black
With hollow cheekbones of stone.
At the end of the long day
The leaves rattle
And I remember the sabra-boy with the guitar.

PART III

THE DREAM OF STAIRS

46   *Ballad*

I wish, I wait. I wait and I wish.
The fish swims a flick in the sparkling pool.
I know, I hope. I hope and I know
That life is both gentle, both gentle and cruel.

The wind moans, it murmurs. It murmurs and moans.
The fish swims a flick in the sparkling pool.
I wonder, I ponder. I ponder and wonder
That life is both gentle and cruel.

He came, he went. He went and he came.
The fish swims a flick in the sparkling pool.
I linger, I hunger. I hunger and linger,
For life is both gentle and cruel.

He loved, he loathed. He loathed and he loved
The fish swims a flick in the sparkling pool.
I tremble, I sorrow. I sorrow and tremble.
For life is both gentle and cruel.

I accept, I rebel. I rebel and accept.
The fish swims a flick in the sparkling pool.
I marvel, I suffer. I suffer and marvel,
For life is both gentle and cruel.

47 *Meditation*

Take a petal, imprint it on your mind
And you have reached a point of meditation:
It sounds too simple, dangerous and strong
To undergo this odd initiation.
For very soon all unity is broken
By fragments of bright individuation:
A flashing light, a noise, a sudden motion
And you have split the mood of elevation
And trickled from the cup of the sublime
Into the aching prickles of finite time.
Away from the glorious calmness of the static
Into the painful turbulence of the dramatic.
Those who seek the clarity of unity
As opposed to the dimness of community
Will find it in a leaf, a star, a tree,
A sudden glimpse of deep serenity.
Take a petal, imprint it on your mind
And you have reached a point of meditation:
It sounds too simple, dangerous and strong
To undergo this odd initiation.

48 *Duality*

On each shoulder is perched an object.
On my right a dazzling glob of silver
Reflects the world around in microcosm,
Passing faces, a door blown open, the petal of a daisy,
Crystallised into gleaming speckles for ever.
On my left a black and craggy lump,
Opaquely jutting out,
A barrier between myself and the sky,
Looks like coal, but something more insidious,
Sinister shades,
A wilful turning away from the light,
Could be evil, could be an outreaching.

49   *The Dream of Stairs*

A wide expanse of gleaming spirals ripple
Once carved in agony out of human bone.
I hesitate to touch the toothlike ladder.
It greets me with a hideous white leer.
I crumple all my fear into a ball
And tiptoeing high I throw it all aloft.
It swoops clean to the top of the bony height
And flutters down again, a wispy boomerang.
I must awake and breathe the living day.

I kick the ball about on the crumbling ground.
It yoyos happily from side to side
And I am left to bear my feet intact.
I quickly start to climb the grinning stairs.
They groan at every step and softly mutter,
With grinding teeth and cold conspiracy.
I must awake and breathe the living day.

50 Moon-Treasure

At the back of the moon,
Beyond the green cheese
Lies a bad of black ash,
Love never spoken,
Killed by schedule,
Split and sprouting,
Tramples over the black craters,
Wailing, eerie,
Stampedes on all fours,
Growing spiders,
Scream of the wind.
Do not stare too long at the moon
Or you will turn to green cheese.

51   *When the Hands Freeze Cold*

Everyone must bear between their fingers
Icy rods of fear
When the hands freeze cold
At night the black pools of the netherworld
Pull us down
By day the flashing chaos screams in all directions
Stretching us into a Catherine wheel
Of turbulence.

52 *Lost*

Over the hills,
Olive-black trees and wet sky at night,
My voice broke free,
Screaming after the running dog,
Legs rolled up and down in the damp soil,
Like sausages on a machine
And the grass started to revolve
Around and around,
Burning shrieks,
While the black fur darted away behind the leaves.
The sky turned to rubber,
Soft upon the trees swaying,
And the mud of the path sank willingly
Beneath my feet,
A murderous life-shaft,
Released from the cords of day and night.
I screamed and screamed and screamed
Until my voice was flying around the trees
And the night filled my lungs like wet leaves.

53 *Sin*

In the falling away,
Grey wings of bird cloud downwards from the sky,
Lies the separation, wings parting wilfully
From the One Source of Being;
Resting sky high.
Long ago could not see Him, being a part of the whole
Evaporated unity and could feel no pain of
Selfhood cramping limits, fallen, fallen away.
Now from this level the space hangs above and below,
And each bird hovers at a different height,
Conjoined to none.
But if the wings should fail, surprise clipping,
Flapping terror,
Quick spin around to grope at fingers of air,
And to fall, fall through the blue vacuum,
Pricking particles of light,
Drifting deeper to I know not where.

54 *Revelation*

When I tore away the curtain of my pretences,
And saw myself face to face,
No shining spirit,
But dust and flesh and dust,
I realised that my old soul had been a lie.

Naked recognition
Does not come smoothly
But grates upon the longing,
The wish to climb higher.
Only by this quick tearing away into skinless agony
Can I begin the slow ascent uphill.

55 *Concrete Ground*

Cold clatter of feet against the pavement.
Empty grey concrete in the square askew.
When I have stepped over this line
And this one, and this one,
Dizzy succession of cuts upon the stone,
I will have accepted the pain,
The long pain of the endless ground.
Empty space despite the criss-crossed blocks,
The squares that do not fit,
The cracks, the jutting-out pieces of stone,
Upon which I trip.
Whose fault?
Stone, cold stone.
Grey merging into white.
When I have stepped upon this line,
Foot flat across it,
Dissected into two and joined again
By the fragments of stone,
Then will I know
The endless pain.

56   *Neurasthenia*

Virginia saw it too,
The door of the lounge opening sharply
And a crowd of smoke jostling people,
Rose in a vase on the sideboard,
The bald man's moustache glistening with beer,
A mouth opening and shutting with laughter,
Removed from its face.
Dizziness as the colours clash
And scream around my ears.
I do not know which way to move.

57 *Schizophrenia*

The book of my mind lies open
And the left page, the inner world, leads into
The right page of the outer world;
But my book has been chopped in half
And I can only read
The insular left page.

58 *Leucotomy*

They cut a slice out of the brain,
Triangle of water melon,
Swift removal before the computer had managed
To find the right program.
Strange jumble of nerves;
What cannot be understood
Should never be anaesthetised,
But must be endured,
If not by stoicism
Then let the old, slow white days drift past
In obedience to the click of time
And the rise and fall
Of the electrical mind.

59 *Hospital in Winter*

The snow is falling February white
Outside the hospital window,
On a church-bells Sunday afternoon.
Voices.

Will my mother come to visit me?
Won't my mother come to visit me?
My addled brain swoops to the circles of snowflakes.
I see Hell besmattered against the window-pane,
Besmattered against my face, my pain.

Whispering voices are telling me something, telling me.
Please be quiet, I can't hear what you're saying.
A word. Stuck on a word,
A word going round and around.
'Even. Evie. Even.' What does it mean? 'Even. Evie.'

A coal fire is burning in the centre of the long wall,
And a girl is reading a book slumped in an old armchair,
Pink dressing-gown and lanky hair over long shoulders.
She turns round to stare at the door,
A bony face, the face of a horse.

My frozen feet. Rows of white beds stretching far out
On either side of me.
Are there people in the beds? I cannot see them.
Are there people outside the window?
I cannot hear them, but I can hear voices,
A crowd of voices
Screaming outside this castle window, a battle-scene.
Snowflakes and church-bells. Perhaps it is Easter.
No, it is too early.
Not yet time for the white Easter Sunday.

Nobody will come to visit me
Snowflakes falling.

60 *Disillusionment*

I have scrubbed the house from top to bottom,
Sponged away the dust and dirt,
The balls of hair and the cobwebs
With a steaming cloth of acid,
And peeled away the paintwork by mistake.
Germless,
Inoffensive,
Non-idiosyncratic,
And I wish I had not done it.

61 *Percentage*

So many gaps,
White patches, which I should have painted
And words I should have spoken.
The morning after
The mind serves to redress the balance
By filling in the loopholes and the crevices,
So that in reflection
The memory is unified, perfected.
To accept a life of fifty per cent is difficult.
To think in totality is impossible.
Somewhere between I throw a coil
And lasso together the fragments with the whole.
A release of energy as polar opposites are conjoined.
An explosion of atoms into the mushroom fallout
Of realisation.

62 *Regret*

Cut out with regret,
Pull back into the basket of the womb,
Kill with a light speedier than time,
That turns somersault
And undoes in a cartwheel of breech birth
What should never have grown to flame.
A love grew
Weighty with surprise.
It burnt away contentment,
It made vulnerable the perception,
Which used to measure by hours,
But now calculates in gripped recollections.
Cut out with regret,
Kill with a light speedier than time,
What should never have grown to flame.

63 *Change*

The girl with the operated nose
Walks along the city street,
Smiles thankyou to the glances
At the beauty which she does not own
And wonders whether she would rather
Be herself again and alone.
Drills drumming along the crowded streets,
As buildings are operated upon by cranes,
Milling crowds weave through the scaffolding,
Dodging this way and that,
And all is subject to change.
A falling ladder and a heap of bricks
Could crush her bones to disfigurement,
And the change would seem a natural law.
Why then this guilt at the slither of bone
Peeled away by a surgeon's knife?
The tiny scars on the skin barely visible
Throb in her head,
An echo of the scars to her loving self,
Which the old face inflicted.

A year ago today,
I walked down the streets alone,
White pavements on all sides and no-one smiled.
The frosty sun tingled against the shop windows
And weeds sprung up round the trees in the damp soil.
I could see the cord, that strung the weeds to the sun,
And I could hear a thundering silence, lingering peace.
Today the streets are crowded,
Bobbing bodies, laughing lips,
Sentences shuffle in the air
And a street accordion vibrates against the window-pane,
But I have lost the cord, that bound the weeds to the sun,
And I cannot see the damp soil
Or hear the thundering silence.

64 *Onion*

I have peeled off the façade,
Wrenching off the onion-skin brown wrapping,
Crisp tatters
And the trickling flesh beneath
Makes me want to cry.
Perhaps with each passing year I shall shed a new skin,
Caterpillar rhythm,
Sporadic stretching.
Only nine lives are given.
Should a core be found beneath the white rings,
Will it be myself
Integer?

65 *Giving*

Can never give enough,
As much as I would wish
Of myself to others.
Convoluted umbrella
I point to apex,
The utmost of effort,
The peak I seek
Daily,
But never reach.
Invisible gap of steel,
Slice between magnet and knife,
Before they jump together and touch,
Cannot be pierced without dangerous
Fusion.

66   *The Madwoman*

There is a madwoman gaunt and brown
Sitting by the carriage door,
Her hair is lank, her eyes are dull.
Her cheekbones hollow, her clothes are poor.
Sitting by the carriage door.
Soon she moves to make room for more.

We pass a suburb, it flickers by,
Time flickers by and smoke flickers by,
And through the wisps of its dusky glow
She begins to show signs of a strange elation,
Unusual and manic, an elevation,
Static, ecstatic, the joy of madness,
The joy of meaningless contemplation.
It has no meaning, no rational meaning,
And is unrelated to external location.
It just follows the rhythm of her own metabolism,
Up and down. The train slows down,
And we have arrived at our destination.

The train slows down and the smoke drifts by.
The woman is quiet and calm as before,
Lank and bleak and gaunt and poor.
Is it vapid sentimentality
Or even the sign of a low mentality
To sympathise were her ebb and flow?
This unsophisticated joy.
Manic and pure,
Meaningless and sure,
Simple to the core.

67 *The Ugly*

Let the ugly speak
In angular smiles,
Distorted glances.
Let them express in a grin of separated teeth
The warmth
That disturbs their ill-matched features
Into a symmetry
Of reconciliation.

68   *Blackbird*

Frozen fingernails turning yellow.
Cold shivers around my shoulder blades.
On a bench in the square,
Legs crossed in beige trousers,
An aeroplane above against the sky,
And in the vacuum between the ground
And my dangling shoe
A blackbird walks on spindly legs,
Scratches its wing, feathers ruffled into a tremble,
Like the cascading notes of a harmonium,
The fluttering ceases and it looks up at me curiously,
Pointed beak upturned like a child.
I could stamp my shoe on it,
Stamp out the trembling before it knew the moment,
Or I could stretch out two fingers, yellowed with cold,
And stroke its black back,
But I know I would recoil.
And so earnestly I watch it,
A slow, calm, maternal gaze.
It twitches its beak in different directions
And, satisfied, disappears behind the bench
And out of sight.

PART IV

FULCRUM

69 *Regeneration*

So I survived and compromised with the mottled ground,
Which beckoned me hither and chased me thither,
And never let me be free.
But I lingered still.
Days come and go in drifting flow
And the straining after looking beyond,
Delving above and below,
Continuously in a mindless yawning cycle;
A still unfinished dress rehearsal,
Never to let me be free.
Sometimes I awake in dreams in deep, deep sleep
And see an excerpt of the real performance,
And then I sleep and love again
The old repetitions.

70 *Wakening*

Morning wakening,
The chalk-white air hanging adrift,
Empty the body and peaceful to float upon
No thought.
A line of waves pulls the body along in a horizontal,
Billow upon billow upon billow,
The pillow gapes in the middle
And the head sinks, the feet each weighed down
By a different rock
Begin to rise and float.
Eyes open to black and brown shapes and white spaces,
A dress thrown over a chair,
The sleeves droop,
Yellow and brown flowers with flecks of green.
Cannot identify these shapes.
Nothing matters.
The network of yesterday has disintegrated.
Chalk-white light. Rolling
Peace.

71   *Vision*

Stretched out in a darkened room
Opposite the orange dazzle of fire,
I wait for the headache to abate,
Tense network of nerves to loosen into coils
In the blackness behind the pink eyelid skin.
A craving to read,
It grows,
To read at full speed, to run headlong
Through a forest of sentences
And fill the restless mind with ideas.
A flicker of orange light,
Will not read, will not read,
Only to think slow thoughts, abstractions.
In the coal-black void I see the visual surface
Crumble away.
Pictures and colours and shapes no longer exist
Only to live, to live, to live,
Bouncing black coils unwind, unroll.
I open my eyes slowly
And as the colours steam into my soft eyes
I am reborn.

72   *The Losing*

I have forgotten it,
The guilt which lay on my back over the years
Like a woollen sack.
The peace that seizes me today
Is a cotton-wool gag
That muffles me and will not let me speak
The burden
Which I dare not remember.

73 *See-Saw*

Life is not symmetrical,
A layer of white icing upon the marzipan,
And a ring of angelica to complete the design.
For the wrongs, which I commit daily,
I cannot apologise,
Simply bear the see-saw rejoinder
Of wrongs heaped back on me,
And hope that somewhere between the two planks
Lies a fulcrum.

74 *Fulcrum*

If I could sink down into my stomach
And fall to rest upon a red velvet throne,
I would become my offspring and my master,
Silently to supervise day in, day out,
The child that feeds upon me.
No one knows where the centre lies:
Perhaps at this place, nodding to sleep
Upon the soft tufts of crimson,
Locked tightly within this black velvet cave,
Knowing only the dreadful waiting
For each moment to turn into the next:
Here lies the fulcrum.

75   *Keyboard*

There is a test-card C of selfhood,
Shades of happiness or worse.
Check the grey and black panels to find
The level at which you are really yourself,
And return to that key
As often as you dare,
So that you may spend
As much of your life as possible
At the correct pitch,
Day after day.

76   *Time Suspended*

Now that the pendulum has swung forward
To six o'clock summer,
Time lies suspended, spinning upon an axis
Of three o'clock,
Trapped in the middle of the office, where I sit,
Trapped in the shaft of sun upon the screw of my watch.
In this limbo anything can happen.
Far away the memory of winter,
The broken geyser in the bathroom,
And the lumps of ice and dirt-fleece
Upon the rim of the overnight glaze
On the bedside table.
Now that summer has melted us into the wallflowers,
Blazing blood-red on the windowsill,
We do not hurry or worry
Or think any more,
In this timeless wave of summer heat.
At this moment the grains of black markings
On the wooden desk
Gleam with polish and perspiration
Beneath my arm stretched out upon the wood.
Fragments of conversation
Spin around in a Catherine-wheel,
Spikes jutting out, overlapping at the edges,
Thoughts unfinished and unexplained
Will never be resolved, never, ever be explained.

A vacuum of time
That houses the breathing and the furniture of this room,
The shimmer of heat and trickle of sweat,
The sweat trickles, trickles down my arm,
Back into time,
Back through the needlepoint of light
On the screw of my watch
And the tips of the minute-hand.
A tick and a click
As the hands begin to move again,
Pulled back into the pool,
Magnetised to perform again
Their inescapable, unfinished drifting.

77   *Yoga Dance*

Yoga dance,
Fly away to the north and the south
Arms and legs gone I know not where,
Energy grows here.
I am one
With the ground below and all spaces;
There is evil in me.
I see it black as coal, a hard lump.
It glitters with silver spots.
Wrench it out
Of the spider cartwheel,
As I turn and flow,
There is emptiness here and aching –
Swallow it up.
The pink flesh will accept it whole
With curved palms
Pulling inwards
Dizzy cup of fear
Drink up the pain
And flow.

78 *The Vision*

Smile upon us, lazy beauty,
Out of custom, out of duty.
You need no hard-earned profession,
You exist on self-expression.
Smile with iridescent glow
On us poor, weary men below.

We have travelled far to find you.
Do our tired eyed remind you
Of yourself before your fame?
Though we moan, we do not blame
You for your leisurely existence
Just reward our long persistence.

Smile upon us, lazy beauty,
Out of custom, out of duty.
You need no hard-earned profession,
You exist on self-expression.
Smile with iridescent glow
On us poor, weary men below.

79 *Song of a Schizophrenic Monk*

What is the use of this strained sensibility
That aches and propels me towards infinity?
Mind-destructive, it yearns for an unfound sublimity
Ruinous to my remnants of sanity.
Sometimes momentarily relenting
I am released from this cruel dementing
Lingering longing for true affinity
With the one true symbol of deep-felt unity.

Weekdays pass in this odd community
Attitudes renewed and stances discarded,
A once fine intellect sadly retarded
By splitting trends in a crazed personality.

What is the use of this strained sensibility
That aches and propels me towards infinity?
Mind-destructive it yearns for an unfound sublimity
Ruinous to my remnants of sanity.

80 *The Singer*

Her voice hit the air with a subtle sweep,
Swallowed up the silence that had been,
Engulfed the fragments of physical existence
And the particles of air floating serene
And bound them together
Into one long, smooth bow of sound.

They listened satisfied as the old profound
Unanswered questions were resolved simple and straight.
No questions left to ask, though some still were
And all was understood like a long-standing joke.

Now the voice is changing, brittle, uneasy,
Communicating anguish, discontent,
And they are left so angry at this deceit
At losing one true moment, which had seemed complete.

81   *Heat*

Heat dissolves me, frees the barriers
Between my selfhood and the rest.
Cold makes me conscious of my tiny ego
In one small frame for ever compressed.
Heat expands me, melts me, frees me
To the fourth dimension, which never fails to please me.

Why do I wish to rejoin the world
From which I am parted by this body of bone?
My hands touch the chair, which rests by the table.
Once contact is reached, you are never alone.
The fire is wholesome and orange and good.
It warms my body and renews my selfhood.

The murmuring flames are cruel to the coal.
They eat it, devour it with torture refined.
One man's sorrow is another's reward
And coal is inferior breathing no mind.
So let heat expand me, meet me and free me
To the fourth dimension, which may yet redeem me.

82 *Nail Armour*

The torn fingernail, which you will pull off
In spite of itself
Grappled with its parent-body and will not be removed.
Magnetic loyalty,
Conventional adherence.
Cannot live and grow outside the flesh-roots,
So hangs on,
Vestigial organ of a former animal.
Man had once a coat of nail
Before God changed it
Into a sheath of skin,
Regrets its melting
And will go back to the old brittle armour of pearl.

83   *The Waiting*

The black days,
Metallic white sky clinking upon stone pavements,
When no thoughts arise;
Only a waiting in the head
For a hand to pull you out of the vacuum
Into the foam of bubble-movement.
Primitive variety of colours,
Fragile skins
That will burst surely.
An illusion, that softens the knife-edge
Between the merging of sky and stone
And prevents pulsating explosion.

No-one here,
Not a soul,
No-one here.
The monk in his cell,
Weeds creeping inside the grey stone,
Could not be more alone
Than this furnace of waiting.
Long ago, when the dinosaur stepped out,
Wriggled over the boulders,

There was air and white sky.
When the molecule rolled away
From the atoms all around,
It charged into a new area of space.
Now the streets are crowded
With the light of sun and moon.
People are lollipops along the pavements
And shops that dazzle,
A thousand theatres, new facades,
Old paint flaking away from hooded eyes
In gallery frames,
Watchful,
Derived from the electrical skulls
Buried long ago in Florence and The Hague.
They tell of a journey that must be taken,
A long tightrope through time and space,
Along with the dinosaurs,
And the weeds twining into the crevices of the abbey,
That will not let go, never let go their cling,
Growing thicker, stronger,
While inside the monk waits alone,
Here he is alone
In a furnace of silence and grey stone.

In the tube
Light hangs from bare bulbs and black squares
Reflecting my face alone in the window;
Outside
The tunnels scream into a game of running.
Here the long upholstered benches lie in wait,
A no-man's land,
Empty as waiting rooms,
That lead in dreams to strange halls crowded with faces,
Smiling, grinning.
Here there are only vertical lines upon the planked floor,
Lines that are lines
And nothing more
And never will be,
Grey with screws of steel that gleam like stars
To bear away the eyes.

This hour is every hour,
Waiting for what can
Never come to pass.
The concrete and glass outside bring no comfort,
Nor the sweep of bird-flutter across in a diagonal.
Slowly
The sun burns an electric star
On top of the rood opposite
Against the white metal of sky.

84 *Lizard*

In another life
Many transmigrations ago
I was a lizard.
Unthinking wriggling indolence
Among the Palaeolithic ferns
And rivers of ooze,
To squelch in whatever direction whim chose,
To stretch out, coils extended over the damp grass
And think a blue sky.
This strange change
Not easy to live a human,
Schematic thought unnatural.
Want to return to my old horny skin
And cast off this soft, pink flesh.

85 *Feathers*

Today,
Floating on an eiderdown of sunshine,
Feathers drifting out, softly twirling,
I smile at the sun-shadows, curled up in my chair.
Across the room the girl on the telephone
Makes plans for an abortion
With cool practicality,
Bony fingers wired against the telephone chords,
Shrill voice echoes the tinkle,
As she puts the receive down.
If only I could share it, her shock, her plans, her fear,
Bottled up like the body inside her.
The surgeon will pare the foetus away with a knife,
And the embryo will disappear,
And the more I unwind into sleepy indolence,
The more she stiffens to protect the unborn child
From dismemberment.

86   *Nightmare*

To wake up from a three o'clock nightmare
Of a Black Mass –
Two men cross-legged
In front of steaming bowls of liquid,
Chanting smoke and shadows,
In a huge oak-beamed hall;
People drifting slowly towards the door,
Manipulated by some devilish charm;
To wake up in the brain-ticking silence
Of the box bedroom,
Unbreathable black air,
Old thoughts rolling over and over,
Until the heaviness begins to evaporate
Into the release of dawn.

87 *The Bag*

Bought on an impulse,
It cost three days of summer dust
And weighed down
With the bulk of cream and red leather.
The shopkeeper had reduced the price by half,
Fatigued by the woman's rusted face,
As she wavered in the shadows of the shop,
The alcoves of the afternoon heat.
Out of doors
The handles clung softly,
Sickening as coach upholstery,
Impregnated with petrol fumes,
That bounce along hygienic journeys
In the dazzle of sky and field and open road.
Soon she knew the bag would be discarded
Along with sentences spoken out of turn
And thoughts
Too turbulent to bear recollection.

88   *The Open Door*

Cannot live glad hours all the time,
Red cushions and sparkling wine.
Must know the throb of the no-way-out,
The surprise of old deeds turned sour.
Cannot breathe the fresh air every day,
Must gulp at open train doors, wind rushing by;
And the eye-smarting grit a reminder of
Old atoms falling away and turning enemy.

89 *Illusion*

You would like me better
If the grey ghost of sadness flickered around my face,
Binding me to you with my need,
A transparent gauze.
Instead I feel the cut of happiness,
That wells up irrepressibly every day
With the green leaves, the wallflowers
And the jostle of the crowds.
I cannot deny my exuberance:
The morning jokes, the lazy afternoon.
But sometimes in the evenings at nine o'clock or so,
When the bubbles of day have simmered away,
The grey ghost of sadness flickers round my face,
And I belong to you.

90   *Nocturne*

Midnight in my square bedsitter
With the electric fire aflame,
An orange iced-lolly frozen into heat,
The splutter of hidden water within the geyser,
A pop song next door splintered
Into three sounds by a faulty needle.
I should be asleep, cut off from the squeal of the night,
But the black sky outside is a friend
Whom I cannot bear to leave.
Wakefulness is a luxury,
When there is no need for action.
I will make my life as useful as the dented kettle,
Silver-grey upon the tiny stove.
The fire scorches, the gas ring hisses,
But the geyser is silent
And I wait for a sign that this craving
Curved arrow of the heart
Will be acknowledged.

91 *Poetry*

To run into a long tunnel, blackness, cannot breathe
And write the subconscious helter-skelter out
Into the blue-green sky-trees open air,
A world of white tablecloths, pass the salt please
And live for a patch of non-think refreshment,
Until the ticking mounts to an alarm-clock signal,
Time once again to dive into the tunnel,
Behind pink eyelids let the brain-thoughts pour over
Into words.

92   *Skull-Light*

The God in my head is more real
Than the traffic-lights' winking rubies
On a Sunday morning.
They will be wiped off that face
A starlight's throw from now.
While the God in my head
Will go ticking on
In the molten lava
Of the grinning earth
For ever.

93 *Selfhood*

There is no cure for being one person
And not two or three,
No way to puncture the skin
And let the self out and the air in,
No quick route to becoming an atom in the universe.
Each day the words fly to and fro,
Linking together two bodies of brain.
The grey cells crinkle with thoughts blended.
There is no way to evade
The silent shine of the sun on the pavements
Clinking beneath your heels,
As you move through the air
Locked in a bottle of skin.

I slip away from his magnetic force every day,
Shaken up by fragments of colour and telephone calls.
If only I could stay
Locked within the black shape of fear,
The fear of Him, that makes me tremble
And shake back into humility,
Away from the fluorescent lights
And the gimmicks of leisure
Into the cold rock-being of selfhood.

94 *Spider*

You are a spider flashing out silks,
A crochet network of your whims and fancies
A symmetrical design praised by many,
And often displayed in exhibitions.
Yet I see in the crossings of thread
A multitude of tiny flies caught and squashed
To reinforce the joints of the meshwork
With their dead bodies.

95   *Interval*

Sleep in wonder.
Do not know where the soul goes;
Hushed to its Father
Or under the earth,
Evil, washed out in the shadows of the window-sill,
Bleached into the white dawn,
Falling like salt
In streaks
Around the drifting bedroom;
Trembles
Between the leaping colours of morning
And in the momentary death,
Hanging,
The balance is steady.
Weighted down with all the love
That wings around the room.
Strange eyes in dreams,
Black as Lethe,
Call you back.

PART V

SHELL

96 *Shell*

I am a shell
Catching echoes of the past
And pearl-flashes of the future.
Satisfaction pervades me in an iridescent glow.
Yet I am brittle and low.
I have withstood the flow of the years
With my strange protective exterior,
But I am flimsy and insecure:
A kick will send me flying down the beach
Into the beckoning sea
And I will return thinner and more battered than before.
For I am insecure
And my beauty is lent by the flickering sunlight
And the swirling whorls of my interior.
The sea to me superior
Whispers and gurgles in its immensity,
But I do not wish to be crusted into pulp
And to merge with the drifting sand beneath the sea.
No. I wish to be free and whole and me.

97 *Love*

My heart like frozen seaweed hangs suspended
Upon the iceberg of the silent river,
Until a wave of love arrives to free it
From the newly melted tentacles for ever.

It spreads its flattened form upon the ripples
Of the water bubbling chill on the hidden ice,
Content with the slow resolving of its motion,
Retarded by the snow on the water's face.

When suddenly a breeze arrives to pull it
Far away from the frozen depths of that location:
It flutters into movement swimming smoothly,
Now active after years of cold stagnation.

98 *Creation*

Two decades and a half have passed,
The spider's silk is spinning fast.
And you bear a child in your silent womb,
Your child needs care, mine understanding.
Two decades and a half have passed,
The spider's silk is spinning fast.

Many years have flashed since vacuum,
Many years to tick till judgement,
Still the problem needs resolving,
Yours needs care, mine understanding.
Two decades and a half have passed,
The spider's silk is spinning fast.

99 *Fear*

No one
Can wipe out the fear that is within you.
Though you collect around you a large circle of friends
To lean upon, each with a different handle,
Still the points of light make you blink in fright,
The silver rings flash against your vision,
Swirling dizziness.
Nothing
Can assuage your unrest,
Though you block out the overhanging shadows,
The clash of colour.
With each obstacle overcome
A new enemy appears on the horizon,
The farther out to sea you travel.
Only accept this black unrest,
Breathe deeply, rocking with the waves,
Grey tongues lashing,
And be discomforted.

100 *Conviction*

I lay on the garden hammock
Stared up at the sky
And tried to pretend that there was no God.
And all over the city people were leading separate lives,
Unlinked and to no purpose.
I chopped the population into pieces with a wire grill
And saw a fragmented swarm;
But as I stared back at the sky,
Soft cotton wool frozen into infinite benevolence,
I was not convinced,
And slowly the wire-grill disappeared
And the people were joined together again
Into a compound of love.

101 *Being*

Fallen away
From the old God-love-bond,
Black iron bar magnet,
Splinter in my heart,
That pricks and makes it tick.
Today,
Free as blue clouds,
I see the space of breathing
And wonder
Where is the core.

102 *Energy*

Every day
Springs forth twins
From the womb kaleidoscope.
Leaves form chains.
We are all one and growing.
The sap
Juice twines between poles apart.
If one day
Can coil two rows of words,
What will the next day bring?
Who will emerge and who will be lost,
Scowled aside
By a downward wish
Of the will turned awry.
In that moment of choosing,
Flicker to the left or right,
Whether to take the stretching outwards
Reach towards some light
Through the funnel
Yellow flicker;
In that moment of choosing,
The day grows twins,
Amoeba divides,
Impulse of outreach.
We are all one and growing.

103 *Pulse*

Stay attuned to the forces of life,
Revolving wheel hub circle,
Merry-go-round and spin daily.
Feel here the slow rub grind
Of falling leaves, that endless flow
Will not let go,
Magnet to hold blue-back
The streak of sky,
Where silent lies,
That used to grow,
Crushed by the flow,
That wants to be let out,
Go, go,
Stay attuned to the flow
And grow
To be saved
From the green-edged teeth of flame,
Where dragons grin in hellfire
Pain,
To resolve the washed days,
That slipped into the drain, the flow,
Long ago, spotlight hours,
That live on in remembered shame
And grow.

104 *Continue*

Pass on to the next.
It grows.
Dandelion clock puffs spiders;
Cornflower swirls
Will be a new figure on tomorrow's mirror.
Cannot believe the looking-glass retina
That sees
Each new two eyes upon a nose
Differently the next hour
From any other.
Words scatter four hours from now.
In this evening's café
Alphabet noodles in the soup
Chew into different reproaches
Around the linen table.
Why cannot they be all one friendly chewing soul?
Instead,
Split into fenced people,
Acids
Blow up the pasta
Into flesh.
Do not know,
Cannot believe and yet should know,
That on tomorrow's mirror
A new figure will appear.
Pass on to the next.

105 *Puppet*

I am a puppet,
Jerking one and two and three and four
In time to the command.
My wooden cheeks gleam in the daylight
And I weep hygienic tears,
Because I want to be loved by everyone,
Not just one or two or three,
But every puppet that jerks beneath the sun.
They creak through this robot world,
Teeth clacking, arms cracking and feet snapping,
In time to the daily performance.
I cry hygienic tears with my varnished eyes,
Because there is only one other puppet,
Who with his fist-cracking skill, can pull the strings
To release me from this stiff rhythm
Into a graceful dance.
And so each time I clatter through the crowds
And barricades of wooden figures,
I long for a glimpse of the strange puppet-man,
Who alone can turn me into flesh and blood.

106 *Nature*

Nature often belies living experience
And living experience is often belied by time.
What comes is felt. It passes and dissolves
Into a fragment as tiny as this rhyme.
A mass of wadding lies between the grains
Of living matter, which alone endure.
These minute sparks elude my searching hand
And drift away according to their law.
I try in vain to grasp at entity,
But when I trap an atom it explodes.
Destruction snatches up my outstretched arm
And I know all too well what death forebodes.
Oh let me be content with what is here
In its familiar state, nor try to pierce
The smoke of gloom which delicately veils
The form of entity alive and fierce.

107 *Ago*

The broken-down fire
Fuses the flat at dawn
Into an older winter.
Red flares across the snow,
As the moon treads heavily.
Soon the wolves will sing and howl,
The curves of ice will sweep across the earth,
The hulk of sky and mountaintops
Will spin into sleep.
No-one cares.
Alone
The bodies in caves
Wait for the whining to abate
And roast back into black comfort,
Breathing like metronomes
To balance
The terror
Out there.

108 *Tunnel*

One soul was lost.
It went tumbling down the hill,
A green hoop,
Stalk-tender shining on the bend
Of light,
Ringing in the air
Basel and garlic and thyme.
It lay curved in the stomach of a child
And slipped over the edge of the square world
Before Galileo demolished it.
I will swim through fire,
Orange and gold, peeling
Into blood
And out of humanity
To find again
After the long coffin-race
Eyes burnished with
Understanding.

109 *Maternity*

On this afternoon,
Tranquil gold,
I would like to have children.
I feel a swelling and a ruffle of feathers.
I will protect,
Teach them my hard-won peace,
Unravelling year by year the secret of flight.
Yellow layers of four o'clock.
All over London mothers are wiping
Grey soap-suds off red fingers.
They pause and listen to the silence of sleeping children.
I, too, share the unknown with the unknowing,
Who have not yet come to birth,
But lie sleeping in beds of yellow seed
Within my womb.

110   *No Mother*

Fear of motherhood.
A broken glass does not matter,
Can be replaced by our own goodwill,
But not the soft fontanelle and the incessant cry.
Unknown cause of complaint.
Total dependence, desire for explanation
Of its own discomfort,
Reassurance that, in fact, there is no need to wail.
Cushioned reconciliation.
This I cannot give
Knowing not myself.
I see the world through a magnifying glass,
Each pore of conflict multiplied by ten.
My future baby is to me the macrocosm.
I cannot console it.

111 *Development*

Baby breathing, mother peeping
Doctor smiling, baby sleeping,
Noise and peace in rhythmic flow
Form that human embryo.

Stories, music, liquid, babbling,
Laughter, clapping anger, squabbling
Noise and peace in rhythmic flow
Form that human embryo.

When he reaches adult status
Makes that sudden, cruel hiatus,
Leaving simple childhood dream life,
Pushing, striving, marrying dream wife.

Age comes slowly, dropping sweetly,
Contemplates his death maturely,
Noise and peace in rhythmic flow
Shapes that immortal embryo.

112   *Release*

The girl in purple trousers lay on the carpet,
Pressed down against the ground,
Willing herself away from the encounter group,
Shut her eyes into blackness.
A hand prodding her in the ribs
Broke through the barrier,
A gasp and then a strangulated cry,
As the coal-fire of tears broke through the black air,
Down, down, down into the past,
The flames flicker against the black coals,
The flames of the love she felt
And the blackness of his silence.
The waves of sobbing scream out,
Body sinking deeper into the hard floor,
Falling into the past,
Until all the blackness is expelled
And there is only weeping.

113 *The Talents*

To pay back in energy
The gift I have been given:
Upon the kitchen table seven chocolate pennies
Wrapped in gold
And a chocolate sixpence.
My daughter fiddles with the first,
Methodically unwraps the gold skin,
A slither of silver curls up from underneath.
She eats with upturned eyes, her face is solemn.
I see that each chocolate is a decade,
And I have only four more pennies to go and a sixpence,
To reach my span.
She plays with the pennies.
Endless possibilities for her.
I put them in a row.
My one goal
In recompense of natural egotism,
I will repay with work upon work upon work,
No limits to my labour,
Until I have consumed myself,
Melted away the last drippings of chocolate.

114 *Decision*

Where the will lies
Flicker to the right and the left
The candle might blink
Out of the tunnel
An eye
Open sight
Distinguishes volition,
Goes this way,
Turns back
But does not know the impetus.
In recollecting loses;
Will be one again
When oblique
It stumbles
Through
Shutters.

He made a decision at that point of time,
Feet dabbling in the sunlight squares,
Reflection of the open window,
To refer all moments and decisions
To the will of God,
To lasso all future experience,
Rope after rope,
Coil after coil
Catching a retreating figure here
And there a falling tree-trunk,
Before the act is completed.
Strange free-will
For is it so?
He will never know
Whether this moment of choice
Was his choosing
Or predetermined,
Before his brain began to spin.

PART VI

WATER

115   *Twentieth Century*

I am a child of the twentieth century;
I have found no hammock to hide in,
No cause to separate me from these unsettled times,
And as the century fragments,
So do I split, ebb and flow.

I am become the twentieth century
And if I live to be old, old,
So will the century flood over
Into the twenty-first
And we will trickle away together.

116 *Individuation*

I hear an inner thump and must express
The useless Weltschmerz and the emptiness,
The flow of a million minds, where thought and void
In alternating patterns weave and blend
A melody of insight and distress,
Confusing to all human speculation,
Unanswerable to close investigation.
Only the powers above can sift and mend
The whirled confusion of that deep recess,
And only the strength of truth can heal and bless
The strange divergent ways to which we trend,
And to God Himself will I confirm
When I finally reach my destined end.

117 *Tryptich*

To hear sometimes the grey groan of the Cross,
Sometimes the whisper that no redemption is possible,
To hear sometimes the weeping of the six million,
Sometimes the whisper that their suffering was in vain;
These are the whispers I hear on either side
As the coach shoots along the dusty avenues of trees
In the flickering morning sunlight.
Birches, oaks and willows
Crackle against the window-panes in loops and tangles
And I foresee a world
Crazily overgrown by trees and people,
Where what is believed is often untrue,
And what is untrue is often successful.

118 *Question*

The Man on the Cross, He rose,
Who knows whether this is true?
For no-one alive has the Methuselah memory
To look back and weep in recall.
But I see every day
A man from his pinnacle of pain
Stretch out to reach God and come to life again,
Mysterious conversion.
And so I believe sometimes,
And sometimes I do not believe,
And in my doubt I find a pinnacle so high
That I think I can never reach the top
And be reborn again.

Was Jesus sad,
When He hung with sad eyes exalting,
Black wells of knowing
And reached out through the thin air to the voice above,
Or was it the voice in His head?
Was He mad,
When He soothed centuries of half-people with promises,
And gave them placebos of a black-tunnel world to come?
Am I false
If I drift into the blue particles of sunlit water,
Salt sand yellow ripples,
And through the clusters of pearl-blue-veined shells
I see in the glints of silver,
That He is there?
Was He mad, selfless mistake unending,
And am I false
In my obstinate wishing?

119 *Devils*

When I was fifteen,
I stood in front of a painting by Breughel,
The lid of Hell and a thousand seething demons,
Thick red splashes of paint mingled with lurid greens.
Today I see beneath your smiling face a thousand hatreds,
And behind the cupboard in the attic,
The flesh of a dead rat is mouldering away
Into sticky decay,
And I am too busy to keep track
Of my devilled thoughts, as they wriggle by,
Or to incite the demons that are dehydrated
And polished back into respectability.

120 *Duel*

Twin pawns of ivory on a chessboard,
Good and evil, black and white;
And when after a complex strategy.
Brain move upon brain move,
Good wins.
The battle is still waiting for the next game.

121 *Twins*

She laughed. 'I looked out of the window just now
And saw two girls in yellow shirts.
They both patted their hair at the same time.'
Her mouth opened into a black slit,
Eyes rolling from right to left,
Trying to grasp it;
Brown pupils like marbles
Seeking to crash against the giant ball,
And bouncing back in vain.
I looked through the sunlit window,
Trying to locate the yellow shirts,
But saw instead my face reflected back,
Black slit mouth, eyes rolling,
And wondered whether the two girls
Had been watching us.

122 *Spur*

I have nothing,
Unless I have all.
The perpetual falling short
Pinches me harder and harder,
Until I have reached as far as I can go,
Almost a peace of wry resignation,
That soon dwindles into a fraction of what I seek.

123 *Holocaust*

'There is an answer to every problem,
If you look hard enough,'
Said the blond boy, thin lips glistening behind gold beard.
But I see so many people rubbing together unhappily,
The patterns that go awry and cannot be endured
Except by evasion.
Perhaps in times of danger he always rushes
To the nearest fire-escape
And never looks back to stare
At the burning blood-pools and screaming bodies,
Face to face.

124 *Conflict*

The soul searcher
Lays aside his pen
And watches the plastic mosaic on the restaurant table,
Blue leaves and orange bells
Against a background of yellow;
The artist's aim
To fit the colours into the right shapes
And draw the eyes into a pattern of contentment,
That leaves no room for speculation.
If only he could exchange his see-saw stance
Of right and wrong
For the skill of a finished visual product,
Which knows that final flash of aesthetic relief,
Denied to him by his refusal to rest at any conclusion.

125 *Reclamation*

Wish to be reclaimed by the Spirit
Now that I am unravelled by doubts.
Want to be resolved into certainty,
Now that my eyes splay to the left and right,
Will cling to the wish.
Will wish a stronger want.
My want I recognise as a need.
But valid none the less.
The gap in me
A vestigial organ withered, which was once
A healthy limb.

126 *Doubt*

They are mocking the devils within me,
The little gold gods that sit upon high in judgement.
They have seen the mouldering fungus beneath my shell.
If I could recover the old gold of solid rock,
And laugh at the sun,
I would do so willingly.
But I am bound to the rock of selfhood
And must grin and bear the mumble and nidge
Of the mocking black spirits within me.
They gnaw away at my entrails,
Not all the day long, by no means,
But sometimes in the butterlight of midday,
When I would wish to share the peaceful glow
Of the little gold gods upon high,
They probe and niggle.

127 *Panorama*

A swarm of birds fly fanlike overhead
And I cannot keep track of them.
Endless directions. Weltschmerz.
In a flash of memory
I see a woman ironing shirts
In a kibbutz laundry-hut.
The steel heat sweeps to and fro
Creating a new crease to blot out the old,
And no one watches.
Damp air rises over the white cloth.
Fresh cotton threads between the yellowing buttons.
Through the windows above, a Wedgwood sky
Burns down onto a crescent of avocado trees
And no-one counts the number.

128 *Corrupt*

I am a turnip gone mouldy
And my top is falling off.
I am vinegar turned sour
And I am valued now more highly
Than before as sparkling wine,
But I know that I am lost.
I am a fungus, rare delicacy,
And I would like to find again
The old molecular groupings
That strung me together long ago
And go back, back.

129 *Black Star*

Black star
Make me strong
Against the pale of night.
Hide from me no yawning caves
In this moment of time beyond the clock
Nothing shall be draped aside
To save the soul from shock,
For the white stars have turned black,
And the moon is hidden
By my knowing what lies beyond the shine
Of nocturnal quiet.
The shadows have cracked away
And the clouds gape open
To show
The dizzy pulling towards some other star,
That cannot be seen,
Black star
That may seem evil
Because it brings the terror
Of screaming darkness,
Expose her hidden places
And shine upon all that is truthful,
The prick
Of being.

130 *Awakening*

The day I put away the tranquillisers
I awoke to a scream of colour, sharp-edged cars
Racing down the road
And tiny printed letters
Jumping out at me from newspapers.
A band of steel cut into my forehead, clanging adrenalin
Running riot inside my brain,
As I walked over the classic pavement
With jerky stops, surprised at the rolling air,
The stone of the ground.
People flitted past as lightly on all sides,
And I could not help smiling without my happy pills.

131 *Water*

Thirst.
A crystal glass ball of ice-cold water,
Salt pain, salt thirst, salt parching salt.
To sway blood pounding in the temples, hot and cold.
If only cold water, iced water, melted icebergs,
Pouring down in rivulets into long-tunnelled glasses,
Crystal facets, rainbow streaked.
Rainbows caught and frozen and melted
Into long, long gulps, long gulps of icy water.
If the desert sun beat down, sand all around,
Dune stretches on all sides, far, far away on all sides
And no hope of water,
How could I bear it?
The soldier in the battlefield, alone,
Hidden between the trenches,
Would like to drink once more,
But fears that cold water will never come, never,
No water, never, no crystal transparency,
Only the opaque streaks of mud, brown and sticky,
Lingering.

The Man on the Cross knew that water would not come.
He gasped and grasped it. He accepted it.
The poet, when thoughts are scarce,
Shrivels up. He fears that ideas will never come, never.
A drought, a parching thirst, a vacuum.
Thirst.
A crystal glass ball of iced-cold water.
Salt pain, salt thirst, salt parching salt.
Perhaps cold water, iced water will never come,
No, will never come,
Never.

132 *Weep Before God, Laugh Before Men*

Weep before God
When the ice breaks through, snaps brittle surface of crust
And the black chill of water
Underneath bubbles into fiery heat,
When into the driftwards of the underworld
You are sucked,
Never to know the answer,
And laugh before men,
Golden hearts swollen to love-burst,
For the brown sinews are friendly
And grip you into peace,
When the old jokes of long acquaintance pull you back
Into the magnetic field.
Weep before God, when the blackness in your heart
Drags you into the terror of endless floating,
The Hell of listening to the brain-tick
Each moment growing large
As it rises to fall into the next beat of time
And laugh before men,
As they multiply day by day,
Searching and loving, pins on the tiny point of a magnet,
Floating around the vacuum of this huge constellation.

133 *Suicide*

A glass of water and a tube of monotonous pills.
Pearls of death to kill you,
But not to resolve your problems.
These linger on annoyingly after your body has died
And the mortals who remain in compromising life
Must resolve these as well as attend to
Your dreary funeral.

A buzzing in your ears and a palpitating heart.
Unconsciousness is near.
Lingering death is not for you nor pain, you hope.
But to take the easy way out
You weaken in drugged oblivion and die.
You coward
And fool.
Yet deserving of much compassion and understanding.

I fear not death,
For it sifts life's soggy bread and milk
Into curds and whey.
My dead self will attain either nothingness
Or complete unity with the universe,
And then I will be at peace.

It is life's ambiguity,
Shadow upon meaningless shadow,
Which I hate and dread.
The hostile face, the twisted accusing finger,
The love ignored or ridiculed,
Too quickly fed,
The relentless complexity of new day and new tomorrow.

Therefore weak, but resolute,
He jumped into the black river,
Purged of momentary hesitation by the scorching
Ice ripples,
And choking bitter waters.

134 *Silence*

White dots in the air
That fizzle
And want to speak.
The silence pounds noisily against my ears.
I hear the wheeze of breathing,
Crackling hair, soft swish of sleeves against the chair.
I stand poised, a stone within a catapult,
About to be hurled into speech;
Pulled back
As the master hand of reticence presses me down
Into thundering silence.

PART VII

THE NINGO PIN

135 *Chawton House*

In Chawton House, the birthplace of Jane Austen,
Regency symmetry, peace and elegance intermingle,
White walls, a ballroom dress, a hanging tapestry,
A creaking door 'purposely left, so that Jane
Should have warning of approaching visitors.
And could put away the manuscript in hand'.
Why so?
When today the manuscript is the only part of her
That has survived?
Her inner life revealed to the queuing public
Could not be disclosed
To the passing relatives outside her door;
Or perhaps the intrusion
Would have jolted her back into reality
Away from her tasteful moulding, transformation
Of the muffled scenes behind the creaking door.

136   *She Searched for Happiness*

She searched for happiness
As if it were her right.
The right of a woman
To live and to be.

She searched for happiness
Wishing for the right.
The right of women
To enjoy and luxuriate.

She searched for happiness
Which was her right.
But needless to say
She did not find it.

137 *Alien*

You, who dwell in a cold and Nordic region,
A stagnant place, where nothing is forgiven,
Release me from my pity and my sorrow
And come back home. We'll bear you no derision.
Nothing is mocked at here; no one will stare,
I hate to think you'll wither and age out there.

We know you and we love you
While you stayed here,
We asked no questions, probed you with no glances,
Be what you will. Come home, all is forgiven
And make this life a pleasant bridge to Heaven
For now you ache and suffer far away,
Loathing yourself in meaningless dismay.

The day you went away my heart was shattered.
It crumbled into many prickling pieces,
Each time I think of you I weep and shudder
And my regret renews and still increases.
Nothing is mocked at here; no one will stare.
I hate to think you'll wither and age out there.

138 *Afterwards*

Is this an eternal waking,
After the eye has shut onto death,
Waiting for what can
Never come to pass;
No ear to hear diversion,
No wrist to stretch out to another?

Now
The blank screen remembers
The whole face
Of the past.
Primeval and cave black
It reflects back to the present,
Like two mirrors astride opposite walls
Dwindled into silver shadows.

Now the whole
Tumultuous course of events.
That formed one life
Must be unravelled
Before it can find peace.

139 *Shock*

This death
I cannot quite believe in.
Cannot believe in at all.
She will come walking into the room tomorrow
Surely,
Face crumpled pin with laughter,
Arms swaying sideways,
Brisk clump of footsteps,
Cannot believe that in silence she lies
In a wooden box, hidden ground-deep
And I will never see her again,
Ever.

140 *To Grieve*

Cannot feel a proper sorrow,
Cannot reach back to the black source of being
That will whisper the words of grief to me for
This death so sudden.
Only surprise and a twinge of remorse
For my numbness,
As though this had lopped off the tall stem,
Chopped into two stalks
A life that was reaching out, growing.
Now at last the black waves
Curve upwards and roll over me,
And I grieve for the person that lived,
And for the second person that will never be,
Perhaps somewhere,
Condensed in blackness,
But never unravelled with the slow white life-years.

141 *Grief*

On the corner of the arcade
Between the mahogany display
And the vases of spring flowers,
A woman in suede is fierce with tears.
Her face has cracked into triangles and points,
And the brown leathery skin, once smart,
Is now shiny and sodden.
Her jaunt habit of walking still remains
To mock her heavy shoulders and neck craned forwards,
Hiding the twisted shock,
And I alone at this split second of time
Know that she has lost someone, something,
Black gloves crumpled into the palm of her hand,
Something that can never again be recovered.

142 *Roses*

At three o'clock
The line that cuts the afternoon in two,
The roses begin to fall.
They have fallen every year of my life.
I see them fall in the garden of four-years old
Fall beneath the blackening storm-sky,
When the rain tumbled down onto a white silk handbag.
They fall outside the long windows
Of the college dining-hall
Fall in sunlight patterns, that fix
The silent girls frozen over their motionless hands
For ever,
Strange silver sunlight that makes them sombre.
And now they fall, pink scattering saucers,
Onto a figure walking down the path.
I may never see him again,
Perhaps once or twice,
But never as before,
When the sweep of bush-roses fluttered down
Pulling us away with their coral scent,
Away to the original source,
Where there was no scattering of showerburst,
But only the compressed ball of clutched flowers,
As they once grew in the beginning
Before the Fall.

143 *Return*

I felt myself falling through a hole in the ground,
Down, down into the gloom,
The terror of dizzy dropping,
Sick lurching of the heart,
As the white hole at the top
Grows further and further away
And the hope of reaching light again
Diminishes.
Trapped in the gloom with my empty mind
I reach at last the soft earth at the bottom
To confront myself face to face,
The gloom at the base of my being
And sink with relief into the springy soil
Able to breathe again.

It came back to me,
After days of waiting,
Surged slowly back to touch the cliffs,
And I was filled once more
With the knowing.
Long minutes of spiky-edged waiting
Pressed into concertina flat folds of time-doubt,
Compared with the moments of
                hours of
                days of
Feeling Him there.

144 *I Wonder What This Constellation Will Be*

I wonder what this constellation will be
Five eras from now?
Will my vibrations still be roaming
Around the black sky
Along with a myriad of others,
Notes in a gigantic silent symphony,
And my bones fossilised into chemical components
Of the earth?
Will there be anywhere – a spot, a shadow –
Which I can call me?
My thoughts to live on in the dreams
Of clairvoyant sleepers
To flash through the nightly hum
Of all that has ever been?
And will my words be remembered by some God,
Who, if He exists, will think from time to time
Of one idiosyncratic specimen
Who flowed out of His creative release
Black speck among an endless torrent of spawn?

145 *Forwards*

Each one of us
Will one day be broken,
Spirit wrenched aside
As years ago the ship's surgeon
Would saw at wasted limbs,
Hiss of the flesh
Falling away beneath his knife
That could never keep rhythm with the burning shrieks.
One day
When some of the mystery has departed,
Yet still a release of surprise
At the actual moment –
What will happen?

146 *Resurgence*

The empty spaces and wasted days,
Hours frozen by love grown old and decayed,
And minutes paralysed by dust,
Where do they lie, these spaces and places?
Between the grimy cracks of the pavement
That grate and twist, as we tread them down darkly,
Or are they grounded deep into the earth
And crushed back into our bodies,
Lying afloat,
To re-emerge in the seeds of future children
That live out old negative moments
And perform strange, unpredictable deeds?

147 *Gold Door*

There is a gold door in the sky;
However hard I knock
It will not open,
Never open.
Brown cloud told me so.
No it will never open until death
Slowly to reveal the gaping crack.
If I could be content
To tingle with probing knuckles,
Never to crack the surface crust,
Nor scratch the fibres with pins.
On good days,
Slow blow of wind tapping,
I hear soft voices
All around
And feel the yellow metal
Glide beneath my silent palms.

148 *When the Door Opens*

When the door opens
The silence will be broken
The finger-bones of air will filigree to ivory.
Meanwhile the gramophone of memory
Plays out old scenes
Recalled
In waiting;
When the door opens
The speckled lace of air will tear to shreds.
The streets outside wink rubies
Fluorescent over shop façades,
Heels clink like water in a well
And echoes fall away.
If the door will never open,
The room square and frozen
Will be a blind coffin
And play out old gramophone records forever.

149 *Save This Soul*

Save this soul
Catch its dropping
Through the net before it peters away.
Freeze it, consolidate it,
Hold it fast within the iron will
Forever.

150 *The Ningo Pin*

I'll give you a ningo pin,
A pin of God,
A tiny pinnacle of ice,
Minute and scarcely visible,
One end a bulk, a minute swelling,
The other a crystal, pricking point,
A slither of frozen water –
A ningo pin.

It will bring you luck
Wherever you may dwell,
A glowing flicker of superstition
To glitter and twinkle forever,
An echo of the happiness you have known
And all that is yet to come.

One hot summer day
When the scorching sun
Breathes fire on the torrid ground
My pin will melt and trickle away,
A droplet of nullity,
A frozen zero,
A mere shadow of a pin.

151 *Inconsolation*

The death of someone you love,
Unknown agony,
Cannot be consoled,
It is the death of God
And the mystery in them
Will never be discovered.

152 *The Soul*

The human soul floats down from Heaven,
At the dawn of the day of the life's long span
And up again it will later return
To rest in the place where it first began.
Existence is one long procession
Of alternations in human succession.
The actions remain, but the players are new,
A million permutations link
The thoughts of a hundred decades ago
With what today you are tempted to think
In one long unending ebb and flow.
The soul, which rises, must afterwards sink
And the only fact we certainly know
Is that all is resolved as death's circular brink.

153 *Waves*

The waves roll in
Day after day
And beyond the ocean
People grow old.
Grey lace of water,
Fringe of brown lace
Grows old beneath the clinking teacups,
China white as the bones of a skull,
Burnt dry as ivory in the rays of the sun,
Cleaned by salt and pared away,
Bones change to fossils and people decay,
Day after day;
Continual switch from the rocks to the shore,
As the sea edges the cliffs away from the sand,
Burnt away by the pressure of water,
Slowly the cities move and change,
Like snakes coiling up as the years roll by,
The phrases change and alternate
And people move to another land,
Grey lace of water,
Fringe of brown lace
And the waves roll in.

154 *Insight*

The spirit entered them;
Salt smoking a tumbler of water
Could not cloud so much.
Ectoplasm
Against the attic door
Could never creak so much
As their surprised bones
When the spirit entered.
It was not peace;
The frozen evening
Tongued
Their hands into pink leather,
Clenched thumbs and fingers into silken sausages
To keep away the pain.
It was not perception.
The street they walked along was
Heavy,
Cast a gate of shadow.
There was sick surprise
Beneath the glassy wind.
When the spirit entered
There was hesitation.

Hanging cheeks, weigh down with the ache of ideas,
That can never be resolved.
No juxtaposition can bring to balance
The scales that hang awry,
Weighted down
By a curiosity, that is infinite.
Only when by chance
In a pure moment
A vision emerges, that is whole,
Does the mind fall to rest;
The pearl has grown,
Swollen over the speck of sand,
Button of cream and white silk
Glimmers
At the base of the sea,
Frozen into relief.

155 *Preserve*

No one knows,
Where all the energy grows.
The Earth drinks up remnants
Of old hours spent in the spinning of phrases
And movements, that have turned to stone.
The past is locked up like an old film,
The shapes and feelings all, buried alive
Somewhere
In an invisible archive
Kept to preserve the giving moment,
Which was received
Shrivels into seed
And falls away
To grow again later
Into an explosion,
Black grains
Of giving.

156 *Signs*

There are signs,
Strange to interpret, but there to be found,
If you perceive hard enough.
The link once conceived
Grows daily.
A coincidence that multiplies,
A reversal of upheaval
Into order,
The slots fitting together one by one
Into a geometry of peace.
Moments when all is explained
Not verbally or causally
But simply by the light of the bulbs shining down
Onto a group of people,
As they listen to the silence
Between the rise and fall of their conversation.

157 *Belief*

When it is cold and empty,
Black sky,
Blind eye,
I come to you, Lord, frozen
And know that the tiny black speck in the albumen
Will be nourished
And grow to explosion.

158 *Evolution*

This passage along the days,
Does it lead to a greater knowing?
Nights watched by the stars,
That prick the consciousness
Into moments
Of steel delight.
Would a hundred years release some
Impenetrable source?
Or is it a horizontal journey.
Sailing us along,
Lulled into parallel acquiescence.

159 *Anchor-man*

Anchor-man,
Black as the night you are.
Pulling out your boat further across the sea.
You beckon me;
I saw you once in a dream,
Eyes black as Lethe
Calling me back.
The waves rolled over,
Grey tongues lashing.
I do not know who you serve.
Some God perhaps
Or worse.
The days pass by like balloons on a string,
Bright evenings
Punctured by the night,
And always I seek
A little more
The words I choose to speak.
Black as the night you are,
And as the night I do not know you,
But must rest a while to find you.

160 *Reconciliation*

Uncorrupted, He participated,
Tore off the outer skin.
The arm exposed to feel,
White lymph weeping
Vulnerable
To bridge the gap
Between indignant man and God.
No reconciliation ever complete
We ebb and flow between doubt and understanding
A stab of love in recall of His deed, we endure the smell
Of human involvement.
Then distracted by telephone calls into forgetfulness.

161 *Cave God*

At the bottom of my mind's cave
Lies a wedge of darkness,
And here I retreat,
Hollow of deep mud gloom
With glints of gold-ore
Sparkling from the shadows.
In the silence of the self's core
I drag out the atoms of goodness,
That will redeem me.

God's presence is not a crutch
It is the cave I was born in
And my return to it is natural.
Black shadow God,
Who resides in my empty mind
That sinks slowly to the bottom
And finds peace.

162 *Knowledge*

Only God knows the truth
Of the shades that bind and divide us.
Only he knows our duplicity.
I can deceive you,
And sometimes myself.
You can deceive the world
And sometimes your dreams.
But neither of us can deceive Him.

163 *Security*

It does not lie in a house and home,
It does not lie in a mate,
It does not lie in the giving of love,
Nor the absence of conflict and hate.
It lies in the conscious essence of truth,
Which motivates every act,
Resolute selfhood, strong and mature,
Forms a circle, secure and compact.

164   *The Dance*

A ring of friends, arms linked softly
Around supporting shoulders.
Legs curved into a dance
In the heat of orange midnight party lights.
To dance a dance of joy is meaningful,
But this is a dance of rest.
No movement, but the twining of colliding legs,
The slow shuffle and the bony hand,
Which eases the falling arm.
They are supporting each other in the struggle
Against themselves,
Mocking the force, that binds them into a gregarious ring.
Everyone of them would like to ease their way out
Of the tangle of arms and waists and hips,
But the magnet of cushion resting flesh
Is too strong, too linking.
Slowly the circle moves on
And the nodding heads fall together in the centre,
A muted clack.
They smile at the absurdity,
And continue the slow dance of life.

165 *Yellow Flame*

Curiosity infinite
There is much work to be done.
Lest I will never find a destination
But must go
Plaited in three directions
And feel the tangle.
At the end a flame
Flickers yellow.
Gaze joined to the central pulse
No moment will ever be more real than this one
Not before,
Not after.
Now I will go,
Never to reach out of this burnishing
Inside
Yellow flame.

166 *Praise*

God
Spreads his
Warmth and peace
Over the afternoon air.
Now there is much rippling
In transparent golden light of
The sunless bright hours
Between four and five
Praise be to Him,
Who knows how
To release contentment
Into the empty chore,
The laborious action,
Now all things around
Rise up and sing silence.
Like the chirping birds
Outside but frozen into no sound.

167 *Corn Song*

I sang a song of yearning and derision
I sang alone in a field of poppied corn
And the birds stopped singing
And pecking the leafy bushes.
Instead they listened to my song and were intrigued.
The corn-sheaves stretched up high during my singing
To catch the subtle nuances of my meaning.
I sang until my throat began to ache
And the flowers that I was holding
Fluttered to the ground
And my watch stopped ticking,
And the birds started singing
And then I lay down in the corn
And dreamt of poppies.

Epilogue: To Speak

You say everything so explicitly
That the meaning is annihilated.
Words.
What are they but the diminishing of meaning
Into letter-structures?
When our forefathers groaned in caves
And painted blood-red patterns on the rock-walls,
There was no confusion.
So that we may understand each other a little better
Let us keep very silent.
Silent   SSShhh.
SSShhh   Sil—   SShhh.

Inside the Stretch of My Heart

I felt a circle of ears beyond the trees,
A stillness over the olive flower-beds
And I knew in that second
That I was one person,
Locked up inside a bag of pink skin,
Inside the stretch of my heart,
That all the love I had ever felt
Was rolling away down the hillside,
A crowd of shadow-figures from the past
Were toppling away for ever

from *Loss*

PART I

MORNING

1 *Day*

The earth turns rebel against itself
Green satin falls away from the root
The caterpillar tugs off its horny membrane
To the rhythm of the earth-beat,
Pulse of larva cycle
Acorn shells fall away
Each action dislodges the next
Until the course of events
Is pressed together in a concertina hold
And then released
Waves of sound
Like crushed glass
Rolling into the sea.

2 *Journey*

Endless book of days,
Each night follows with pictures of day,
Snatched away
Into truthful distortion.
I read this life
Stretching the muscle of mind
Into new places.
A diamond with many facets
Could not cut as sharply
As these sights overlap
Yet cannot be valued.
Redefined,
I see a clear track.
Train sweeps down the line,
Yet cannot believe that never
Will the journey be perfected;
Can only be read,
A page of days shows sometimes
A good sequence,
But today will be a slippery journey.

3   *Call*

Some eagle hovers overhead
It presages a message.
Steals something away.
Is it my conscience
Beating aside the evil,
Off, away;
Or perhaps a ghost from an old era
When things were wholesome
And fitted into place,
Calling me back,
Back and away,
Back
Back and through?

4   *Time*

Mother breaks through
The barriers
Into the born child.
Mirror cracks the night in two.
Future
Carries down seeds,
To join the first day to the last.
Who knows the past exactly?
Lost,
It comes out sometimes,
In a glance of déjà vu,
Hovers between the lips of clairvoyant speakers,
Surprised by its own power.
No ghost reversing back from the future
Can rattle and groan
To tell of the changes that will come to pass;
They cannot be caught by he shocking speed of light.
Baby smells of warm milk
And wobbles its head.
The broken cords between mother and birth
Jerk back
Into identification.

5   *Waking*

Force open these eyelids shuttered so tightly,
The cinema-screen of a nonsense dream-world.
The morning breezes enter so lightly,
Relieving the dusk of gloom that nightly
Descends on us from the sky uncurled.

Softly adapt yourself to the dawnday,
Shadows of sleep drift over the ceiling,
Where genuine flickers with dream-echoes play
In harmony round every jubilant sunray.
The grey depth of sleep is salted away
By the pure, purging slap of morning's cool sting.

6   *Morning*

Scorching light of day.
White fire
Falls, in a curtain
Onto the streets of London,
Rubs away the shadows and the flame
Of yesterday,
When twilight
Hung heavy as mould
Between the crevices,
Like grass growing in heaps,
Cannot be weeded out.
Now,
Bath of light
Purges
Into bone
The city centre.
Skeleton of ivory
Cannot weep,
Bare-eyes stare
At its nudity.

7 *Monday Morning*

Leap into the white void of Monday morning.
Fill it up with gestures, words,
A layer of grey shingle at the base of a tubular glass,
Craggy stones to bear the weight
Of the diminishing week,
Until the apex of Saturday
Crumbled off into Sunday
And slithers down to the bottom of the funnel once again.

8 *When Morning Is Whiter than Shell*

When morning is whiter than shell
And many moments part towards pain
And hasten to peace
Then do I know
The true mirror
Of myself.

9   *Aversion*

The cat, a seething kettle,
Paws and claws at my clothes,
Bounces back at every push
And curves around the mahogany table legs
Like melted plaster
Head points into the air to take a bite of oxygen
And lifts a bent paw as if wounded,
But I have no sympathy.
The persistence of the intrusion
Negates the docility behind the gurgling purr
And I surprise myself by my aversion
To this patch of furry flesh,
That only wishes to communicate.

10   *Tube-Time*

In the tube
At twenty minutes to nine,
There is no space to breathe.
Only a hedge of bodies, Worzel Gummidges in coats.
Lost in a world of red angora and grey-flecked tweed
I sink back into the past
And fall forward into the end-of-tunnel future,
After the jolting to find a soft destination.
There is no time or space within this place,
No name for it.
Only the chugging along the tunnel
And the stations on either side
Are chopped off, snippeted away
Leaving a clean-cut circle of human cushions.

11 *Nine to Five-Thirty*

Daily routine of
Coil upon coil of workdays,
Springing up, never ending;
Trapping you with tight wire rings,
Which bruise the arms, disallow gymnastics.
Only the bobbing dance of the donkey tied to a stake,
Which mesmerises him into acceptance.

12   *The Bureaucrat*

Circle
Shoes in the morning
Sun white through the gate past the houses up for auction
Train   desk   papers
Three biros   one black   two red
And a pencil going blunt,
Grey flint bulge
Stone eyes of the watchful workers
Locked off into their weekday portholes
Sinking in the afternoon
As the sun snaps into
Six o'clock
Slowly
Very old dust
Train   newspaper   barricade
Through gate
Wash the feet
In soap orange-tan smelling of leather and thyme
Cleansed
No traces   into evening   and fall over
The night
The bed lurches with the
Clock bell
Sun   cold   white   hostile
Through the gate past the houses up for auction
Smell orange leather and tan and
Some spice

Cannot tell
Catch a new face perhaps a slice of news today
Eyes blue as slate
Hot watchful locked in portholes
Submarine nearing land

A square woman
In a tweed suit, brown checks upon the pink
Nothing achieved in her past sixty years
But the weekly paypacket and a long, long line
Of downtrodden subordinates
Having successfully held them under the water
And lashed out at her enemies, her peers
She can now surface to the water's top
With a spiral of bubbles
Lungs unused to the open air, gasping angrily
A lifetime of labour
Energy driven out in all directions
Only to find a long white sky
Upon an empty ocean

13   *Sartoris*

Birds   singing silver
Outside   rain-splashed ground
Inside   office
Papers   files
I wish   I wish   I wish   I wish
For ever
Birds   singing silver
Above the rain-splashed ground

14 *Intercom*

The pigeon coos mercilessly
Outside the office
Pleading for some love
Or turning instead to hypnosis
By repeated strain of winged throat
Inside the concrete and glass
Heads buzz, training
Figures into data
Coil upon coil
Torment and change

15   *Through the Barrier*

No moment will ever be more real than this one.
It is not before,
It is not after.
Morning coffee in the office
Cannot break out of the routine,
Wrench away the bars.
There will never be any walking through
Into a more vital area of emerald fields
And shimmering air,
Tiny yellow flowers that smell of wine,
And eyes that explain all in a pinpoint.
The shadows on the dusty typewriter
Hide the other side
Of living,
That cannot be pierced.
The girl by the window looks out and sighs.
The slink of a spoon against china
Overlaps onto her reality.
Yellow and blue turn to green.
She throws the past and the future
Onto a carpet of black velvet,
Packages wrapped in fancy paper and red ribbon bows
Tumble onto the ripples of gleaming pile.
She is sucked through a funnel of black velvet
Into the pinpoints of dust.
This second is this second.

16 *Paper Children*

Invisible strings
Sweep the squares and corrugated cuttings
Of paper along the pavement.
A yellow tube-ticket flies up in the air
In a trilling spiral
And flickers down again,
Beaten to the ground by the age old
Dominating parent of gravity.

Paper children – green shield stamps and pink receipts,
Blue tissue paper and red chocolate wrappers
Rise up to beat the air in adolescent rebellion.
Only one buff envelope manages to float away,
Down the pavement and round the corner,
Where it is stamped to shreds by a can-kicking
Teenager not recognising
His own reflection in the footmarks.
He mangles it with a screw of the heel
And hurries down the road towards the music shop.

17 *Chain*

Bonds that break and merge
Day in, day out,
The fibres interlinking.
Six workers in an office bound together
By liking, rivalry, civility.
A quarrel. Two threads snap.
A promotion. One more.
Fatigue. Two more.
Only one thread tenuously remains to provide
The nucleus for the renewing
In waves,
Flux
Of bondage
That will re-emerge and unite them all once again.

18   *Communication in Silence*

For four years we have worked in the same building,
A large place,
Often silence.
You superior to me in rank by far,
We have exchanged perhaps ten sentences
Over the past four years
And yet I know you.
I do not know your house, your friends, your family,
Only your stillness.
Quiet thought,
Efficiency.
Yet not mechanical,
Springs from a pious fervour,
The wish to justify daily bread,
Or the belief in the value of effort.
If I stay here for another four years
Or even eight,
We may perhaps exchange another ten sentences,
Or even twenty,
Yet I will never know you any the better.

19 *Dust*

Strange to see this familiar face,
Nothing new,
Old white speckles in the air,
Dust from morning sleep at the ebb of the week,
Silence and dust.
Same voice pulls out
Remembered pictures of summer afternoons.
Growing old in the dust;
The grey steel ebb of another moment
Falling into the next.

20 *Launderette*

The washing-machine's stomach
Is in pain,
Heaves around with clothes.
The people seated on benches at different angles
Of impatience
Listen to the hum and vibration
In anticipation.
They will be here at the same time
Next Sunday morning,
Eagerly awaiting a new birth.

21 *Morning Break*

A typewriter tapping, dust upon my desk
In the shape of an L,
An empty stomach,
Dry itchy skin
From oversleeping.
Reluctantly at work
Out of the office into a pool of lemon sunlight
Filtered through green leaves
In a latchwork. Not computerised
Or mechanised,
But rambling, intricate.
I fetch a carton of milk from the dairy.
The street is dotted with people
Bubbling and laughing.
I stand on the pavement,
Guilt at hunger winning
The conflict of the body and the mind.
I gulp the cold air and pay the penalty,
Thin lashes of sunlight.

22   *Telephone*

The telephone.
Black furry ear
Closes
Into slot,
Black pool of total immersion,
Overlapping vibrations,
That play a tissue tune.
Somewhere
Over the wires,
Between the poles along the tracks.
Stops the voice to gasp
And lose itself against the white metal
Of overhanging sky.
Wind slips across;
A blackbird hovers
And forgets to sing,
Flapping
Wayward confusion.
Here
Lies only
Communication.

23   *Crossed Line*

Listening to two conversations at once,
I gave the wrong answer to each,
Smiled briskly at the weeping girl by my shoulder
And uttered words of sympathy
To the business-caller at the other end
Of the black receiver.
So it is each day
Our minds
Cannot make a note on the jotter for the right call,
Cannot respond to the millions upon millions,
I do not exaggerate,
Of winking eyes and flashes of light around us,
Crossed line.
I can only apologise for this galaxy of confusion.

24 *Moment*

At this moment,
I have curved round the legs of the chair,
And jumped into the Wedgwood mug,
Disintegrated between the jumping
Letters of the newspaper,
Hang in the fuzzy air
And drill outside the window with the crane.
I see the sleeping cows in Dorset
And the apples in the greengrocer's shop
Across the road,
I lie breathing inside my lungs,
Waiting for the ribcage to swell out once more
And topple over into the next contraction.

25 *The Reading*

Hair aflame with the heat,
Eyes gummed up with the sunlight,
Hand dropping over the musty books,
Want to sleep,
Slee-ee-p.
Slowly
Prodded awake by the spiky rows of words,
Black conglomerations of tiny hieroglyphics,
Pretending to be phrases and meanings,
But actually mere pressings of black ink
Against mashed white wood-pulp.
Drop the pretence and
Slee-ee-p.

26   *The Bluffer*

We were talking in a hut on a strange Israeli morning,
The sabra-boy and me
And I regretted to myself
His lack of education, formally I mean,
For his schooling had been little
But by nature so much was there in him
He said that laughing children
Were like stars falling askew from the sky
And I in admiration
Thought everything he spoke was original,
If not profound,
Or so it seemed,
For he had picked it up from those around him,
His phrases and conceptions were copied,
Not self-begotten,
Acquired from men
Whom afterwards I met myself
And then I recognised the source
And they rang hollow.
Why did it matter? Words are words, ideas ideas,
Even though churned out by a second receiver,
And I'm sure the spark of originality was there
In my deceiver, only not so much as I had thought,
It was just a question of degree!

27 *Worms*

When I was young and the rain poured down,
The pavements were cluttered with silky pink worms
That lay straddled in sophisticated coils of contortion
Like weary corpses, except that they were both alive
And also resilient to the splitting stab,
Which instead of annihilating them,
Merely increased their life-force by two hundred per cent.
Today I never notice them, alive, split or otherwise
Perhaps I am not perceptive any more,
Or perhaps growing weary
Of their continual fight for survival
They creep into cracks in the pavement as I go by
And wait for me to overtake them
Before they loop their way out into the open air again
With assumed nonchalance.

28 *Portent*

Over the morning hangs
Third eye,
Cyclops second sight,
Plumply in the middle like a grape
Of bulbous ice.
I will go through.
The night will write a different script
From the printed message of yesterday.
It will mirror bluntly.
Glazed spears of angular disturbance
Will shoot once more
Their gunpowder anger.

Cloud of the afternoon
Grey as an old potato lump
Hangs slantingly;
Portends all that could arise
Unexpected looking-glass
Black shapes march across in flailing rhythm
Strange the directions
Which they can take
Away to the unaccountable places
Only to stay,
Black box of self, packed light as a cube of soiled ice
And never to meet.

29 *Incommunicado*

Three words.
Brief answer to his torrent of affection.
Pursed lips, once red,
Now almost grey in the ten o'clock light
Of Saturday morning.
Cups upon the draining-board are brown
With the stains of old tea.
The waters clings tepidly to her fingers.
Her age now apparent to him. He speaks again,
His arm curved round the edge of the kitchen steps,
Expansive, hopeful.
Three words.
Brief answer. He droops.

30   *Torpor*

In the antique shop on the corner,
The bald head of the shopkeeper
Is bent over a rail of old rugs,
Red and ginger flowers, threadbare greens,
And the cream ear upside down does not hear
The tinkle of the door, as I enter.
A jingle of light music is jogging up and down,
Vibrating the three vases on the window-sill,
Yellow, blue and green.
I spear the frozen shell of glass with an invisible finger
Racing impatience, as people walk by outside the window
And I am trapped by the lockjaw crouch
Of the silent old man;
But slowly, infected by his torpor I dissolve
And fall to rest inside the blue cave-bowl
Of the vase in the middle,
Particles of sea and sky.

PART II

MIDDAY

31 *Living-Room*

Blue cushions,
Plumped out,
Smug,
As duck's breasts
Upon the carpet.
I will not be deceived
By the midday sunlight,
That transforms the living-room
Into lemon stillness.
The sea is grey and salty,
When it flicks lashes
Of mud into dead fish.
This dry room,
Heated,
Painted hangings,
Is not here.
It is a slowly built makepiece
To hide
The sky of ice
And wet twilights,
Which really sting.

32 Ugliness

We met on a blistering summer's noonday
On a bench in the glare of a sweltering park.
I was afraid of him, he was a stranger
And also he happened to be rather ugly.
I had to sit near him for lack of space
And I was afraid of his unpleasant face
So strong is the force of conventional attitude
But he chatted away with agreeable platitude
So that his aura of strangeness departed
And I became friendly and almost warm-hearted
And his gleaming white teeth also reassured me,
They were part of the benevolent forces that be.
The very next week I met him in town,
Out of the blue and quite unexpectedly,
He, unaware of me, wore a bleak frown
And I was revolted all over again,
Though I tried not to be, not to be, not to be.
Then once again he revealed a white grin
And my world was restored to focus again
To its old satisfactory congruity.

33 *The Boast*

The boast
Spilled out of my lips
In the hot sunlight.
Bubbled with energy
And ten surprised eyes
Stared back at me,
Small black points against pale cheeks.
I wanted to pull the sentence back,
Like a yoyo on a cord.
But it was too late.
The thoughts had grown and burst like a soap bubble
Flat against the grained wood of the desk,
Its seeds now distasteful
Like the scum of old soap.

34 *Fishes*

Sitting at twin tables
I see
Your white seamed lips, twin fishes, smiling
Surprisingly,
Where I did not expect it.
Your table, a solid block of brown wood,
Has frizzled to gold in the sun
And midday has dazzled a shoal of painted fishes
Over my head.
I am lightbound and unstrung.
We are twin people.
Why then do you curve into a smile,
When all I can feel inside the golden net of my head
Is blackness?
You are the pain inside my hollow head,
The mud, where the golden fishes used to swim.
Why then do you smile, white seamed lips,
Tiny bubbles of calm knowing,
When all I can feel is the frizzle
Of scorched fishes inside this black bowl of dust?

35 *Summer*

Wallflowers scorching blood in July
And the mother knitting
Tipped steel together
Clinks
Like whistling gnats
Out there on the sun lounge
The girl
Clamps back
The weight of her love for him
Which unexpressed
Now lies scorched into the field of grass
Where ghosts creep around in fear
That all will soon be over.

36   *Bubble*

At one o'clock,
Head swollen to a bubble,
People milling on either side were cardboard figures,
Burnt into the golden air,
Trapped by the smiles all around
In a time sandwich between morning and afternoon;
Nothing could touch them,
And the cars that swept along the road
Flick away the dust, that had settled on the black tarmac,
So that the ground was brushed clean of decay.

37   *Lunchtime*

Walking one by one
Down the white concrete blocks of kerbside,
I see such shiny rectangles on all sides,
Rushing past.
There is always the moving onwards,
Even the grey flecks on the ground jerk zigzag
Beneath my shrinking eyes
And pedestrians sweep past,
Curl around the shops like heaps of dandelions,
Carelessly bent with the weight of shopping baskets.
No silence in the coughing air
No stillness in the shuffle of wacky phrases,
The wind against the double glazing
At the end of the street a four-storey tower
Rises high, a whitewashed crack against the water sky
And sways.
No-one is ever motionless
No city ever rests at any time,
Not even a flat patch of parkland.
Each stone vibrates,
Seeks to reach out,
Just as I do now,
Through the opaque brain
To someone in the city, someone I love.

Cellophane sandwiches, cold sausages and brown apples,
Boots shuffle to the counter,
Camel-hair elbow prods to the front,
Crinkle of hairs pink
Against the spoons.
Outside lorries grumble
From Holborn to Surbiton and back again.
A dog weaves through the queue,
Whirs its head
And totters out into the blind light.
Fingers prod a totem of stitches onto plastic handles.

38   *Crowd*

Brown and pink arms
And faces,
Rushing to catch buses,
Teeth aglow in haste,
But not smiling;
Perambulators in Brixton
Roll over squares of paper.
A yellow plastic bag
Upon a pushchair
Crossing the road
On wheels of silver.
I remember now all the evil,
That is in me,
It rises up like a pebble,
Black and shiny.
A shopkeeper's angry voice re-echoes
Beneath the yawn of buses.
The crowd
Moves forward
Like a centipede,
Unrepentant.

Hate to be in a crowd
Hands pressing on all sides,
Indented fingers in my back,
An elbow upon my buttock.
Degradation abnormal,
Yet is this so?
Perhaps the truth of concentration-camp normality,
Bodies no longer individual,
Artificial self-respect for the box of air we walk in.
Now
Shame and distaste annihilated
Along with six million Jews,
I forget my body
And subsist.

39 *The Blind Man*

Rush-hour malaise.
Slow plodding of feet on all sides
Through the tunnel. Hypnotised
By the rhythmical tread, thighs jerking up and down,
Puppets we advance, a day of boredom stretching ahead,
Our senses silenced.
In the middle of the crowd a blind man
Chats eagerly to his escort.
'Tim took his bicycle to the garage this morning.'
Attempts to be normal, one sense lacking,
Vivacious.
Perhaps his belief in God necessitated and justified.
We respond to him as a friend,
No longer barricaded against each other,
Victims of the rat-race.
A stab of love kindled by his white stick
And by his ignorance that with faculties intact
Harmony comes seldom.

40 *Off Peak*

In the peak of the rush-hour
The man sat down next to me,
Squat, fat and jostling.
Broke a tacit rule
And chewed his fingers.
Then with a file,
He scraped the nail.
White slithers.
Dull fatigue, off peak I watched
In hatred.
Then a decision. The choice of free will,
I decided to like him,
To switch the will into a different gear,
Like the antennae aerial of a television set.
To push the steel rods down to the left
With a quick motion.
I began to like him
And as the crumbling nail-dust
Rolled off onto his trousers,
Flake upon white flake,
So my hatred diminished
Into a clean-cut half-moon of civility.

41   *The Joke*

A man and a woman in a restaurant,
Waiting for coffee.
He joked.
She sighed. It was more of a wail than a laugh,
A scream of pain
To see the link between the two ideas,
The normal coin and its counterside, the absurd
Crudely interwoven.
Her laughter was loud
To crush all future attempts
At such cool impudence,
Breaking the horizontal line of her day
From morning to noon to evening to night,
Each portion linked with squares, different yet fitting,
Pastel greens and blues of a patchwork quilt,
To keep the sleeper warm.
Not a moth-eaten old fur coat
Thrown over the blankets by mistake.
No taste, so primitive, so underbred.
He will not make the same mistake again.

42 *The Bore*

I thought of you, picking grapes,
The white glow of skin hot upon lucid green,
And as I picked I sucked one grape from every bunch
To test for sweetness.
Gradually I reached the end of the fence of vines,
And the sugar began to grow sour against my tongue,
Cloying acid.

43 *Kibbutz*

Lime teeth,
Straw of grass,
Stunned beneath the fanwater,
As the hose pours down.
Could I shed this chalk skin,
Peel off into brown health,
Like the women in sun-chairs on the lawn,
Chattering,
Arms and elbows fat,
Move around evading babies?
Sun, hot-glazed behind the Wedgwood sky
Crackles the avocado tree
And weeds that prickle
Beneath long toes.
Men move slowly from place to place
Dangling long bodies, tiny hips
And swinging from lazy shoulders.
Hot dust melts,
Cotton shifts, dry soft,
Cling folds;
Reach out
Loops of guttural laughter,
Quacks the argument in half.
Criss-cross of lime and earth-clods,
Scorched huts on the patchwork,
As the kibbutz
Burns new friends
Onto its open face.

44 *Vacuum*

In a café by a window
There is no thought.
Transparent mind mirrors the world outside,
Jumps off the edge of the world,
Topples over from the corner of the square earth
Before Galileo demolished it.
Down into the black smoke
I dissolve into the tight threads
Of the blue linen tablecloth
And smudge the filigree plant pot window
With my collapsing atoms,
That permit this anachronism.

45   *Trafalgar*

Pause,
While London changes,
Here in the central square
The fountains
Lift a gleaming dish of Trafalgar water
To placate some Anglo Saxon god
Baffled
At this usurping traffic;
Streams of hoodlums perched astride
The pepper and salt stone
Defy the thrust
Of spiked water-gates,
That will never let through the sixteenth century,
While nearby
In walled galleries,
Huge colour snapshots
Linger on forever
In heavy frames.

46   *Outsize*

The fat shopper in the fitting-room
Stares at her contorted self in the glass.
Her wishful eyes, like lenses, narrow the bulges
To plumpness,
And then as the retina readjusts,
Invincible accuracy of the optic nerve,
She sees again the curves of rubbery pink,
That dent at the touch
And then fill out again,
Like sandcastles sinking in the sea.
They assert their validity
Despite the prospect of hunger-cramping weeks to follow
And her angry sigh as she squeezes out
Of the much too little black dress,
Reminds her that in a different century
This swollen goodness
Might have been recognised as such.

47 *The Enemy*

The challenge of an enemy,
To recognise the black shadow that approaches
And step calmly onto its surface.
Do not be deceived,
When the dark outline fades into the twilight,
A treacherous invisibility,
Convinces you that animosity is not your problem,
Your warm, frank smile and a life of channelled effort.
But the shadow will return beneath the hot sun
Of beating midday,
Black against the white sand.

PART III

AFTERNOON

48   *A Flock of Blackbirds*

A flock of blackbirds
They cry and cry
And turn and turn about the sky
They fall down on the brown fields
Where the farmer's plough
Has turned the worms
And up they fly
Blackbirds
In a crowd
I hear them call
I see them all.

The wind is blowing on my window
And a voice seems to come from nowhere.

49   *Dragons' Teeth*

After the broad road,
White as a pillar of salt,
Where the taxi throws a black hearse portent
Into the dust of the lunch-hour hush,
Back to the office;
The typewriters lined like dragons' teeth,
Wary and waiting.
The clerks blackened by fatigue,
Patter and flick of the wrists,
Knit a pattern,
Plain as looped handwriting
And pearl as the spots of sunlight
On the polished legs
And cornered tabletops.

50   *Street Dance*

The crazy sect are dancing
Along the corner of Oxford Street.
It is four o'clock on a Wednesday afternoon.
Why do they dance and sign and jingle bells,
Trailing their pink robes along the dust-tracks
Left by the swish of wooden sandals?
Why do they flick their wrists
And nod their bald heads
Into a row of shaven sandy pumpkins,
When everyone in the offices above
Is cramped within the magnetic sphere
Of individual braincells
Ticking the minutes away?
Here in the streets a few passers-by chat hurriedly
And up there in the executive suite
The secretaries swap streaks of conversation,
Lassoing one personality onto another,
But here on the corner the whole group of dancers
Have lost their selfhood
In the clacking feet of communal jollification.
Bells jingle up and down
And there is nothing left to do but laugh
At the splash of pink robes that sway to and fro endlessly
Like goblins clamped to a gigantic metronome.

51 *Stifled*

Tepid afternoon tea-leaf air
Fills the nostrils.
Two girls, drowsing over their typewriters,
Fling the windows open wider
To let in a finger of same-temperature breeze,
Cannot be felt or smelt.
Unrefreshed, they breathe deeper,
Reassured by the placebo
And wonder whether this is the C-major scale of living,
Which they too often evade
And find again with the stale nod of familiarity.

52   *Friday Afternoons*

Untidy Friday afternoons,
Ends of withered roots sprouting anew
Seeds
For the following week,
Unconcluded. Slow fatigue
Aching neck, backbone extended.
To flop into Saturday
The wish
Dwindles
Beneath letters to type, forms to amend.
A joke. Slow to understand
The laugh.
Convulsions of giggles like the spiral
Of an old jack-in-the-box.
A lorry passes.
Spiky details of bureaucracy
No longer matter.

53 *Interruption*

Bank holiday Monday, white afternoon, no milk.
The Indian grocers on the corner always open.
Teenage boys of graded height serving
And filling up the trays lethargically.
I stand by the till and hand over a five-pound note.
Three silver coins for change.
My outstretched palm touches the till,
Mesmerising him to open it again.
Slowly the crisp green and white paper
Crackles in his hand,
And the jagged teeth grin unevenly
Beneath black dot eyes
And oily black hair.
He wakens into laughter at this challenge
And kicks the spicy bags of yellow grain at his feet.
Green leaf aromas blend into the tepid air
And a man runs past the window pulling a barking dog.

54   Bank Holiday

The park on Easter Monday
Is dripping green
From oily trees,
That clamour into a rustle of drops
Over the path of stones;
Scrape of heels against
A dragging perambulator
And crunched decisions
To spend more time in the open air,
Away from the boxes of brick,
That leak stifled air
And never grow warm,
While here the silvered flesh
Gleams like peach fish
Against flapping raincoats
And little boys screeching to kill.
Now
The third eye opens
To hear a trail of bouncing footsteps,
Which will never
Ever
Reach their destination.
There is a splintering of wood
Into benches of planks,
That hold secure,
And whistling birds
Too wind-shaken
To be afraid of satiation.

55   Park-Time

Sunday afternoon.
Out of the glass-porched house,
Down the high street.
Empty,
Whispering solitude,
Into the warm-air park.
Stockinged feet cool against the grass,
Twigs and black lumps of damp soil.
A brass band plays cheerful marches,
Each portion framed by rows of deckchair clapping.
Toes wriggle against a prickly twig.
A girl shouts with laughter,
As a ball is thrown between her legs.
Sustained trumpet roar of military climax,
As the old week dies and with sharp birth pangs,
A new week emerges.

56 *Rainy Day in the Tourist Season*

Through bleary latticework of rain
The trees in stilts yawn up to stretch
A Wedgwood willow pattern against the glass plate
Of the city square.
Inside the gallery
St Peter lifts up a heavy key,
And the air is filled with Kentucky surprise
And gold frescoes;
At the other end of the town
The traffic is waterlogged into a tight jam,
A circle of grey blocks beneath the drizzle,
Trapped like a swarm of rats.

57   *Misunderstanding*

The coach is flashing through the hills
In the grinding heat.
'Open the door. I'm stifling,'
Shouts an indignant voice from the left.
'Leave it shut. I don't like the draught,'
The old woman splutters.
An arm swings the door open and emerald green
Floods into the mouldering pool of sunlight by my feet.
'It's draughty,' growls the old woman.
I stare at her absently, thinking of
The overlapping speckles of green and yellow.
A Van Gogh two o'clock
Is blazing through the open door.
She intercepts my stare
And her eyes, strange violets,
Throw a pool of suave indignation
Onto my lap,
Sparkling.
'It's not my fault I'm old and feel the draught.'

58   *Shadows*

I have known you in another life.
I delve down to the roots of some pleasant land
Before this womb's existence.
Green fields and shapeless pink huts,
Sunlight and the smell of wallflowers.
Silence of the afternoon.
The fresh winds blow
Into the empty spaces.
I see you shambling aimlessly across the grass
And then through a sheet of shadows
A cold winter,
And your slow movements as you shuffle up and down
Like a caged dog.

59 *Pity*

Pity
Passes through the layered consciousness,
Like butter drenched from cows
In the sunlight;
Speeded up film
Grasps
In one grope through the strings of orange rooftops
Concrete slabs of offices,
Through the ocean of glass water,
Where fish and corpses rot,
Breaks through the night,
The ticking brain,
The thinking eye,
Snaps
Everywhere
In a camera-shot.

60   *Bones*

His anger murdered her with eagle eyes,
Clipped her into white silence.
For three days she was empty,
Dried out to ivory like a bone gleaming dry
On the sands,
Curiously
Clean,
Until the sea released from its freeze,
Jerked back again into rhythm,
And there were new faces beneath the sun.

61   *Meeting*

Changed.
The white skin was still the same,
But the features were compressed, severe,
Throwing away the past in a pinch of breath.
The flame of her rain-blue eyes had flattened into a fish
And ten long years of adulthood
Had left her limpid white.
No rain was falling that October day,
When her shoes clicked into
The old familiar pattern by the kerbside,
A paper's edge away from danger,
Still the same
As the cars groaned by,
While rain moisture hung in the air,
Clung to the steel-white sky,
Impending pain,
And her washed-out skin,
Hollow of thinking cheek and curve of bone,
Grew old,
As I stared, wondering what had caused this alteration.

62   *Fishing*

His poised
Eyes,
Leaping fish.
Fringes of
Curtained eyelashes;
Behind
A small boy waits
To return to the green triangles of fish and weed,
Pull up clods of earth and spiky grass,
Damp smell of mould,
From where the worms curve out
Under the slimy boulders.
Blue iris curved into a marble of water
Looks out
Perplexed,
Middle-aged.

63   *Time Machine*

Red telephone kiosk
Leaning against the waving elm at the corner of the street,
Which of you will fall down first?
Perhaps vandals will remove your panes of glass
From between the red bars,
Or perhaps Century Twenty-One
Will demand a new kiosk colour,
Yellow or turquoise green.
Maybe a storm will crack your branches,
Fractured limbs straddled across the road,
Or a land-development scheme
Will demolish you both with a paper-plan.
If only I could come back and see this corner
In fifty years' time.
If I could only come back and see this corner
In five hundred years' time.

64 *Boredom*

Cold feet on an office afternoon.
Vacant sun shining onto my desk.
Void of thought after an early lunch
And five more hours ahead.
The afternoon asserts itself defiantly.
Choice of subject for thought.
Efficiency suggests a detailed analysis
Of the papers on my desk.
This norm perversely rejected,
The other extreme to be an invisible nun
And think a five-hour prayer.
But no. A lack of conviction.
I let my mind trickle in all directions
To break down the dikes that enclose it.
Perhaps a flood of images
Will swim up from the subconscious sphere,
Strange blackness.
The sun gleams on my hair,
A passive falling down into the pit,
Down, down, down, where no thought is possible,
Only to work mechanically and enjoy
The warm silk of the air flickering against my wrists
In the stillness of the afternoon.

65   *Teatime*

Blue-aproned lady waddles to and fro,
Shoes flapping, forearms
Plump from three decades of polishing,
Hums a song,
Waves in her right hand a rock-solid teacup,
White gleaming against the sodden teacloth,
At four o'clock, her muddled snatches
Of old-time pop songs
For the frisking hour.
Clink and tinkle of teaspoons.
Swish of tea,
Biscuit brown with well-being.

66 *On the Steps*

Sunflayed,
Cross-kneed upon steps,
That fall in piano-layers
Between two buildings,
And a street running between
With an iron gate
Wrought over
With gold upon black;
Smoke and burning kneed,
Threesomes drifting along the flagstones,
And the clap of shoes against stone,
As the cars fleece the roads,
Dustily whining.
White is the sun,
All wishing
Washed away
Against pillars,
Turning the dead Greek faces
Of the building
Into life.

67 *Museum Piece*

Charcoal drawings
Fading into fibres;
Through Venetian blinds
And wired squares of window
Strips of pink blossom
Catch onto birds' wings.
Outside, the May silence
Is punctuated by metallic whistling,
And indoors the buzz of
Hidden heating
Stifles
Into artificial torpor,
Italianate in London;
While clinging to walls
Muscled arms grip spears and nosegays
In bunches of brown ink.

68   Silk-Worm

A jade silkworm in the gallery,
Slippery green glass
From the Chou dynasty,
Takes me back to a pinpoint in the earth,
Centuries ago;
And the mirror of time is cracked
Into the tiny smithereens of jade pottery in this case,
That nail me down with glass pins back into the past.

69 *Growth*

Cats spawn kittens.
Sun ties cellophane of gold
All around.
I read a book, that grows,
Turns me to tree.
I am that book.
Question rises mammoth
To question.
This earth is too small a glove.

70 *Downpour*

Down sticks of rain,
Neck gasping fish,
Eyes bubble-bath.
Trapped in a museum-cased of glass
I see the fish and chip shop
Caught between two picture palaces,
Hacked away slice by slice,
Lie like the old silent movies
Dumbly in skulls,
Beaten back into the earth
By sticks of glass.

71 *Lost Between Stone Basins*

Lost between stone basins
And lions reaching out
To marble stairs.
The museum is so cool;
The perfect place to grow amazed
By turmoil
And concealed doors.
Where keys click into wooden cases
And strong men in black serge
Wind away for ever
Around turnings.
A fountainhead of fear
Pulls away from the crowd
Plaiting queues of enthusiasm
And tries to find the way out.

72 *Age*

This dismembered leg
From an ancient dynasty
Has seen better days.
Now weathered in pink stone,
It sits placidly upon its stand
And waits to be admired,
As it was
Many years before this audience,
An octogenarian,
Who, envious of its immortality,
Coughs a bronchitis sigh
And shuffles away,
Discomforted.

73   *Those Who Do Not Question Much*

Fools
That grin and have faith,
Why did not their matted brains
Grow to such convolutions
As those who scheme
And force their own design
Upon the escaping day?
Those who do not question much
Are carried along by the traffic
That forks through ribbons of trees,
Where the buildings crumble to grey
And tell of the hours
Trapped in the sunlight,
As they wait for the changing patterns of dust
Upon the stone.

74   *Ephraim*

Ephraim in his bedsitter
Smooths out onto grained skin
And moves slowly from chair to chair.
Behind lime curtains
The afternoon
Listens.
The television-set throws two comediennes
Bearing double chins
Onto a heap of textbooks
Below.
A poster of a girl in rags
Above a cricket calendar
Marks the days away
Without surmise.
Only the weekly cheque
To spin along
A new friendship
And clothes of lines and silk
That hang in fine squares
Against the positioned shadows
Of these four walls.

75 *Malaise*

Walking away from the doctor's maisonette,
Through the reconstructed road and the scaffolding,
The surgery to the buildings falling to pieces
Stone by stone,
I remembered the man in the waiting-room,
Baggy trousers flopping against the chair's
Caramel wooden legs,
And the doctor's tired monotone next door.
Through the side-streets the silence
Pounded against my ears,
Despite the crouching boys by the lamp-post,
Playing games with pieces of old branch,
Scratchily against the ground,
Leaving cuts in the soft soil-dust,
Tiny clouds of earth against the wrought-iron gate nearby
And it seemed for a second that all the world
Was mouldering away.

76   *Verdure*

Hatred dwells among people,
Like cheese growing mould,
Turns green,
Corrodes
To old bronze;
Forgotten candlesticks
Unearthed from a Roman site
Can never more spit yellow spears of flame,
But quiescent
Swallow within their stems
The hostile dead,
That hissed
Before their enmity was swollen
To surprised love,
Trapped hypnotic
In the green afternoon light.

77 *Parasite*

In France
The mistletoe sprouts on oak trees
Like birds' nests
Thrown into the branches by mistake
Against the metallic sky;
Lives parasitical and swells guilty.
Falling leaves in autumn
And winter nakedness a reminder
That it must share the bleakness
Of sparse times.

78 *Double Biology*

Thursday afternoons are for double biology,
Green afternoons, like old hot water bottles.
The weather is cloudy April but hot, without ventilation,
And the experiments are slow, plants to be dissected;
A messenger is sent to fetch new specimens
And we wait in silence while the teacher
Moves wrist over wrist the objects around her desk.
The girls in the front row are all in pink stripes,
Pyjama material,
To sleep away this hot water bottle afternoon.
The salamander larvae are swimming round
The brown water of the tank
Between slimy ferns and black twigs,
Shrubs of the waterworld, where all is curling
Away into wriggling life.
Through the window the oak trees swell into
A heap of emerald triangles
And a man pulls his dog sharply around the corner.
We are bottled into this room
And our thoughts wriggle through the air
Like the tiny worms that dazzle the retina
From the afterglow of a white window.
Thursday afternoons are safe and slow
As the teacher moves the objects
Wrist over wrist around her desk
And the salamander larvae dissect the brown water
And move slowly around the black twigs
And under the slimy ferns.

79 *Old Woman*

Scrawny blue-veined hand still clutching
Patent leather navy handbag,
Salmon mac of plastic squeaking
Rhythmically in time to speaking,
Every inch communicating,
Voice and gesture loudly stating
Friendly, yearworn female outlook.

Rumbling down the rainy roadway,
Bus encloses crowded gaggle
Of commonsensical old women,
Compromised to life, but gaily,
Though the body ages sadly,
Triviata compensating
Often loving, rarely hating,
Ugliness accepted gladly.

Acrimonious and bitter she was to me last year,
Her tired feet aching, the weight of years, jealousy,
Now on a summer's afternoon,
Mellowed, her face is an older reflection of mine,
Thin lips, flickering surprise.
Impossible to hate one's mirror,
Every face will echo upon the next,
A microcosm, universal glass,
Woes upon word upon action.
So in silence she walks past,
Forgiving and empty.

80 *Lemon*

On a primrose day in March,
When frost was mindlessly forming on the shrubs
Like bread-mould at the end of a long, stale day,
A whiff of raindrops fell from the sky
And crystallised mid-air into an icy lemon.
Four feet from the ground it hung
In steady levitation
A spray of dust drifting from nearby
Covered it with particles of grit and labelled it
Inedible, unfit for human consumption.
Dusty lemon, I will partake of you,
Though soiled and grimy,
For I need your pungent grip
To teach me a secret.

As soon as I sip the juice
I discover the source of life's vitality.
It lies in a careful balance between waking and sleep
Taut energy and slack leisure,
The thinking will, the contemplating mind,
All is juxtaposed in the invisible hypotenuse of a triangle,
The active and the passive in harmonious antithesis.

The rain is falling silently on a primrose day in March
It washes away the dust and the grime,
Leaving the lemon pure and unobtrusively symmetrical.

81   *To Forestall*

The railway line of life.
Never to be off-guard.
A sunny four o'clock.
Light streams into the green fields,
Yellow fingers of light.
The sheep and the cows asleep.
Vacuum of peace illusive.
Beyond, a rubble of old contorted metal
Wreckage of a car
Thrown onto the line that morning.
A prank or perhaps a crime?
This is the problem of disaster.

82   *Acorn*

When all the love has dwindled away
And sucked you dry as an acorn shell,
Rolling downhill in the dust on a September afternoon,
Clods of earth tumbling in the flickering wind,
The cut of splintering twigs against the ground,
Only then can you feel the empty wind,
Battering blue bulbs of air, unearthly vacuum,
And know that the only thing that endures
Is the kernel point, grit in the nucleus,
Spirit of love that sucks up the dust into a blanket,
A wave of river return.

83 *Saturday Afternoon*

Cricklewood in dust, garbage gleaming in the sun,
Frying like sizzled New York afternoons,
Click over the pavestones
In search of a handbag shop,
Painted blue, that no-one remembers;
Pulled along different streets
By false advice, and caught in a web of sun-steam
And crackling shopping-bags.
The boy in the paper shop
Wrinkles his nose with fluff
And the girl, red-faced over National Health spectacles,
Beams a frank perspiring smile
And shakes her hair over the road,
Two West Indians with raised shoulders
Discuss the sharp guy they met last week,
Cars glint sneering windows
That slip across London out of the zigzag
Documented file of pedestrians,
Whose budgetary achievement is an ideal
To be discarded, when at six o'clock
They leave the streets scattered
Into twosomes and threesomes.
As the traffic falls to rest,
And the coinomatics
Hospitable to the last,
Draw in new clients
Swinging
Polythene corpses.

84   *Bus*

The bus is swamped with raincoats, shopping bags,
Overlapping folded linen gloves and packages of cartons.
The bus conductor, out of temper,
Screams to bulging crowds,
Who usurp illegal stances on the top deck
And around the stairs,
Until after three minutes order prevails again,
Men and women sit in neat rows,
Subdued by their momentary chaos,
Relieved by their confusion
Like children rushing out of school into the neat vicinity
Of drawing-rooms.
Past the windows
Flash shops and neon lights,
Pretty secretaries and scruffy pedestrians.
Silence along the rows of upholstered benches,
The peace of observation as the six o'clock world
Swings past along with the traffic
And the newspaper-sellers,
The quiet anticipation of the evening,
Possibilities of dinner parties, theatre-outings or
Quiet hours spent in front of a black and white box,
Which is as lively as the reality
Along the side-streets and byways.

Suddenly a tramp clambers to the front seat,
Stands bolt upright and declaims religious propaganda,
Hellfire and darkness await for those
Who do not repent.
Titters of mirth among the sleepy rows upon the benches
No condemnation for a drunkard
But pity for his manner,
And yet there is a slow change among their ranks
Of purchases and pleasures,
A faint fear of his sheltered mind
That has been a possibility.

85 *Hunger*

An all-devouring void inside me bleats
And moans for food to fill the empty gap.
Hunger swells a million far-off souls,
We care not, until pain begins to tap
At our own plump selves and then a true
Insight arrives of what they must go through.

When I reach home I'll eat a juicy steak,
Bowls full of creamy soup and fruit to follow.
At present I'm alone in the cruel, grey rain.
Outside I'm chilled and inside a mere hollow.
I never thought I'd feel such misery,
A dreary ache, a demi-agony.

And when I've eaten I will send a cheque
To some worthwhile deserving charity,
And then I'll feel a kind, expansive glow
At helping those who thirst continually.
Meanwhile all my most altruistic wishes
Are drowned in a host of contemplated dishes.

86 *Food-Time*

Taken by surprise
I squirm,
As the man opposite me in the restaurant
Begins to lash out at eating, feet flying in all directions,
Head bent into the plate and elbows protruding;
A splutter and a squeak and a bang on the plate
And he is transformed into a large pink pig,
Flapping ears and curly tail in the air.
The waitress looks at him in surprise,
As his tiny eyes blink
With the dripping of peas onto the floor
And the smoky formica table squelches with mud,
As his palms stretch out exhausted for the next course.

87   *The Waiter*

This restaurant is like a fore-echo
Of an automated world to come.
The waiter serves up each course with clinical precision,
Hovers cautiously watching the last crumb of fish
To be swallowed
And leaps forward to exchange
The old plate for a new one.
I feel like a battery hen
Or a four-year-old,
Whose physical progress
Is a source of constant observation.
In obedience I munch in rhythm with the servings
And leave the restaurant with some of my individuality
Assassinated.

88   The Waitress

You work long, steaming days here
Serving up plates of food
To an ever-changing public that consumes it
Minutes after its preparation.
Who is to prove that you have actually worked here,
When the food and clientele are never twice the same?
Admittedly one pink face may resemble another
And one plate of Yorkshire pudding
Is scarcely different from its neighbour,
And one white-aproned waitress gone like the next.
I know you are the same,
Because I have stamped your card
With weekly efficiency for the past six similar years,
But does anyone else?

89   *Cactus*

Potted plant between the lace of curtains
And fingerlets of frost upon the pane
The years go by for people in restaurants,
Streams of green vegetables turn into days
Of bedsitter waiting;
A cactus life,
As the leaves curl in one upon the other
In overlapping succulence.
Cars outside the window gleam blue and shining
Speeding towards the city centre.
Here on the outskirts
It is peaceful, insulated
And the waiter is always the same,
Once a shy boy, now placid with rotundity
From years of waiting upon pale loiterers,
Who sit and watch the potted plant
Between the lace curtains
And fingerlets of frost upon the pane.

90 *View*

Frost and fog through the windows
Turn the trees to an older decade
Caught leaning at an angle,
Weighed down with leaves and spikes,
Berries jostling in the grass around the trunk
And an old blue door, painted through dusty air
Eternally upon the memory of anyone
Who may care to pass.
Not an atom lost
In the archival chambers of the brain.

91 *Pier*

Walking, windswept
Over the slatted pier
I see the blue beneath the gaps
And above a frozen sky
Of united cloud;
Couples huddled on deckchairs,
Icy smiles on rigid cheeks
My companion takes out a book
And reads on the wooden bench,
Ignoring sea, sky, spray
And I feel
A gust of solitude.

92   *Six o'clock*

Curiously
Relieved I stare at the knife and fork touching at the tip,
Arms pointing together in a demure lap.
Egg and tomato ketchup play Van Gogh
On the plate, and a small frill of grey egg-white
Turns it into a Salvador Dali.
A pop song plays the working day out,
And the drum beat release from the spell
Of routine.

93   Flight

The birds wing jerkily across the mauve dust of the sky,
Where the houses touch the spidery trees.
They gallop away over the curve of the air
And lose all dignity,
Bouncing,
The chords of life broken,
No need to make the primeval journey to the south.
Today they have burst free to swerve wildly
In a star,
High above the railway track,
Watching the incoming trains
Move sleek as a snake down the line.

94   *The Stones*

At certain times of the day,
The time of the stones,
We are alone,
When the waves roll away for westwards down the shore
And the pebbles are naked in the slanting sun rays,
All heaped together in an endless marble upon flint
And always the stones are alone.
It comes when he sees it holds no menace,
Gentle roll of water,
Glint of red veins upon the rocks,
Sweep into the runnels of pounding waves
To discover anew the strange wet sky
Falling into the charcoal water
And the hiss of sizzling chinks of glass
From a broken bottle.
Sweating to bloodboil in the shaft of heat
That brushes down the shingle,
Clink and crunch as the stones fall from the cliffsides
To nestle into a horizontal hold
Clink and crunch as they settle into endless patterns.

PART IV

EVENING

95 *Label*

Walking over the grass on an evening in June,
After the cider in the pub,
With him on one side and her on the other,
Our heads bubbling like marbles,
Opaque though shimmering behind turquoise glass,
I let the seven o'clock sunlight
Simmer into a yellow dazzle and held his hand.
The girl on the other side whispered,
'My God, he's a Hampstead Liberal.
I can't stand them, they get on my nerves.'
She laughed from the corner of her large lips,
And the yellow and green waves of light
Began to settle into spots and shapes,
As my thoughts coagulated into leaves
And blades of grass.
Everything seemed sharpened and minimised,
He was no longer a warm shape at my side,
But a sociological concept
Like the Indians, the Jews, the Anarchists, the refugees,
And as the shapes around me
Solidified into painful clarity, he dissolved.
I turned round to the girl at my side
And smiled back at her
Lopsidedly, in unwanted imitation,
And wondered what would happen
If the wind changed
And my face remained contorted thus forever,
What would she label me?

96 *Summer Evening*

Beyond the footlights of the open-air theatre
Tucked into an alcove of trees,
The puns on stage grow quicker, more raucous
Every moment,
And the wild gulls above
Moan and wail in the wind,
Blocking out the laughing students, the grey scenarios,
And the purple and green satins
Converting *Twelfth Night* into a tragedy of errors.

97 *Tube*

The Tube on a Saturday evening.
No thoughts, only red and yellow jumpers
And a purple coat,
That makes me blink.
The girls opposite giggle
And we are all held down in our seats
By a cloud of warm, smoky air.
No annoyance,
Only a breathing in and out in unison
As the floating colours make nonsense
Of the discarded, thinking week.

98 *Image*

Walking between the great stone buildings of Holborn,
I see in focus
The heavy flagstones
And street-signs in black and white,
The plastic shoes rotating along trays
Through double glazing
And the rain falling softly
On this Saturday evening,
Sweeping clean the revolving doors
And thirsty gutters,
As people in the distance walk in pairs
Heading for drawing-rooms
And pubs and clubs along the way.
I cannot see beyond to the century before this façade,
Or afterwards,
When it will take another posture;
But know only the splash of water
Against rubber heels;
While in another room
The man I love
Sees beyond all this
And shares it with another.

99   *The Evening Class*

The silence has been broken
By a string of sentences, that shuffle out in monotony
Lisping like snakes, that hiss in single
The words rise and flow,
Fall softly around the circle of faces.
The lightbulb pares away the flesh,
Leaving the bones exposed
Beneath its lemon shine;
Grows brighter, as the voices rise in argument;
Brown growl of indignation
Crackles like roast beef,
Performs a startled chirp,
Coughing splutters out like water in an agitated pipeline
And a thin trickle of laughter grows
Until the torrent of conviction
Beneath the hanging ceiling
Quickens and exhausts itself into silence.
A cough;
Space of time to reflect the quiet possibility,
That every idea can be considered in many ways.
The light flickers.

100 *Routine*

No better than the next
We rise and fall;
When evening casts a celluloid
Sheet of brown dust.
Goldfish perceptions flick their fins
Inside the goldfish bowl of mind.
The daily grind
Is a Nazi task
To shift a heap of pebbles up a mound
And pull them down again.
Scapegoating whosoever blocks the path
With idiosyncrasies.
The fish swim around a dizzy circuit
Orange and gold and flecks of green,
Glimpses,
That break through the double glazing of thought
Into the subconscious.
Down there
A black kaleidoscope shapes remembered faces
Into relief.
They mock the day
The glass is sundered,
Waves roll over the crushed splinters
Beneath the roar of traffic
Pouring home
Into the dark night.

101 *No Danger*

Her head is cider-swollen to a bubble,
As she staggers down the road after the concert,
Sleepy in the July torpor,
Ecstatic with the clang of the cymbals of the cantata.
Each step jogs like a burst of trombones
And the lamp-post throws a beam of yellow light
Onto her dilated pupils.
Across the road a familiar voice shouts,
'Come over here. I've got some news.'
Mesmerising her like the bulbs of light,
The clashing chords and amber liquid in the heavy mugs.
A streak of energy shoots through
Like the sizzle of an old battery.
She veers into the road and runs across,
Runs over the bulges of grey ground,
The tiny stones, the warm air.
A flicker of light catches her left eye
And she stops abruptly,
As a car swims down the road towards her.
She stops, hypnotised by the yellow headlights,
That gaze at her with the canny stare of an old frog.
Feeling no danger, drowsy, comfortable,
She looks lovingly at the bulky machine,
As it swims nearer and nearer, faster and faster,
Requesting her to move one way or the other,
But she resists and with a drunken hiccup wills it to swerve.
It veers to the right, submissive but only by law,
And she staggers to the pavement, giggling.

102 *Rosanna*

Rosanna is silent and blonde and haughty,
Her hair swept back into elegant neatness.
Her eyes are round and vacant and black.
Yet she has a meaningless kind of completeness.
Are you jealous? Well, she will not care
For she lives in a silent and cold eerie sphere.

Rosanna is working, mindlessly, quietly,
Working hard in the daytime to celebrate nightly.
Stars twinkle and flash in her empty, black eyes
As she wanders around in a fool's paradise
Are you jealous? Well, she will not care,
For she lives in a silent and cold, eerie sphere.

103 *Foretaste*

Something
Of Hell
I saw
With this woman
Here on the chair
Not in her.
But she knew of it;
Bird tattered whistling,
A fugitive pain,
Alone
In the brown light
That hung over endless
Rounds of space.
Whirring huge,
A scratch of a leaf,
Moaning
From somewhere alone,
Never to know
The next move,
What agony will bring.
Lost for ever and why everywhere
Must drown,
She cannot know,
But only feel;
Her mouth turned down
Not to cry,
And the ache of the huge pallid figure
In the evening room.

104 *Trendy People*

I thought she was* so cool, so untouchable,
Aristocratic chin jutting sideways
Against her green lace dress.
'I don't like them at all,' she said.
'I can't bear trendy people.'
Her eyes, brown almonds,
Glowed nutlike against her pale skin.
In my mind I shouted an angry thought at her:
Stop labelling things! Stop labelling people!
I noted the swollen contours of her cheeks
And catapulted the thought across the air
From my eyes to hers.
I screamed it, I bellowed it in silence.
Slowly she turned away and blushed,
Pink fingers of blood flowing into her throat.
'How silly I am,' she said.
'I don't suppose they're trendy at all.
And if they are, I don't suppose they can help it.'

---

* In an alternative 'second-person' version of this poem, this is written
as: 'I thought you were so cool'.

105 *Hypnosis*

We lay in a circle on the carpet, heads pointing inwards,
A black box tape-recorder held us together,
A man's voice, slow and buzzing, chocolate black
Led us into a cave, where there were no walls
And no exit.
Further along in a horizontal
We were dragged into the gloom until
External thoughts were snipped away,
There was only the centre-point
Of being there.

349

106 *Bio-energetics*

Zany clown,
Red velvet jeans stretching over bony legs,
Leaping on the carpet up and down.
A trick gymnastic to roll away the tension
From the jerky muscles,
To roll away your manhood
And turn you into a goblin figure from a pantomime.
Infectious decadence.
The leaping figures around scream and shout.
The carpet ruffles and purrs
Beneath the long contorted toes,

107 *Last Respects*

Hidden in a telephone kiosk
On an evening in June, green leaves,
One chaffinch singing,
She stared at the red paint
To summon up some grief,
To pray after the death of an aunt. It happened
Two days ago.
Black telephone, a message to the dead,
Red paint and smeared squares of glass,
A pile of directories buzzing with print,
The evening buzzing with eight o'clock exhaustion.
A couple saunter by
Shoulder to shoulder.
There is no sadness, only fatigue.
Inside the flat
The family crowded, chair next to chair,
Laughs and gestures, elbow upon knee,
Shoes crossed, a circle of light gleaming upon
The black leather toe.
Intimacy of blood ties.
No regret,
Only to be united in remembrance of eighty-two years.
'It was a ripe old age.'
The prayers, a long chanting upon chanting,
The surprise of a gradual participation.
A clicking of the wheel into position.

108 *Shyness*

A shy polythene bag
Keeps the washing dry on the way to the launderette
And holds them together in one bundle.
Protection against the sheeting wind,
That could tear apart
The yellow bedspread turquoise sheets
And purple trousers,
Splaying apart the corduroy legs
With the practised ruthlessness of a torture rack;
But locked in their transparent container
They remain neat squares and oblongs,
And bounce together softly,
As I enter the twenty-four-hour launderette.

109 *Interior*

In this Victorian parlour
Eggshell walls and gilt picture frames,
Dust specks on the points of spiky ornaments
And long waxen candles,
That sink cosily into the past;
Within these four walls,
Each objects nestles comfortably into position,
The grand piano gleams and preens itself
Against the bay-window
And the velvet curtains are drawn into overlapping folds
To keep this century out
And preserve the illusion of the past.

110 *Stepping Outside*

Flames and torture-rack of a Tudor epic film
The first cold autumn day hits me,
As I step out of the cinema into Trafalgar Square,
Shaking off my skin
Like a rabbit scuttling out of its hutch
Into a cool bed of lettuce-leaves.
I run down the subway into the tube-station
To talk to a friend
And bury myself in the patchwork conversation,
Trying to obliterate
The band of fear around my forehead.

111 *Surprise*

I do not know whether I have the understanding of sight
All my knowledge drifts through a sieve
Into not knowing;
But sometimes in the black mud evening,
The trees of the city
Hiss and spit, like the pines of an old forest
Meshwork of filigree, that crackles with understanding
And although the green has scorched into black
Charred away into cinders
Beneath the ash-dust lies the whisper
Surprise of growing
That I have known in another life.

PART V

NIGHT

112 *Night*

On the boat pub
Pretentious
Sea curls lashing
Flared light caught
Up
And thrown back
Over
The laughing girls;
Words too fast pour out
Dropped
From the black evening
Quickly
After lager and
Some frankness
Had resolved the civilised game
Now
By the deck
He stares
Pondiferously
At the black mirror
Smithereened
Eyes rounded
The old North star
And a few familiar landmarks
Awaken nostalgia
While she waits
For his mood to change
To workaday good humour.

113 *Loss*

When the dog ran away in the middle of the night,
And through the broken gate and down the hill,
I stood in the garden beneath the bulging black sky
And shouted his name across the blanket of grass.
I felt a circle of ears beyond the trees,
A stillness over the olive flower-beds
And I knew in that second
That I was one person,
Locked up inside a bag of pink skin,
Inside the stretch of my heart,
That all the love I had ever felt
Was rolling away down the hillside,
A crowd of shadow-figures from the past
Were toppling away for ever
And gradually the black sky grew purple with stars,
As the spinning legs of the animal twitched up the hill
And stumbled back into the garden,
Dissolving the frozen magnet of the night
Into a sway of wind.

114 *Winter*

Who loves the grey tent of darkness
At nine o'clock on a winter's night,
When the houses are shaded and silent
And people whisper as they walk the streets,
When the air is soft and sensitive?

I love the shiny reflecting pools
On the muddy pavements crisply ringing
And the puppy, who stumbles and hurries home
To the warmth of a cosy living-room,
An oasis of colour and flickering heat
In the oddly hanging black expanse
Of nine o'clock on a winter's night
When the houses are shaded and silent.

115 *Midnight at the Station*

Midnight at the station,
Shadows disappearing,
Brightly lit carriages,
Journey through cloud and steam,
Crash of grinding wheels,
Onwards,
Bone-shaking over the glassy tracks,
Slits of yellow windows
From passing trains,
Lights pinpointed
From flats across the span of vision,
Lurches to a halt,
Engine still vibrating.
Two youths pause from chatter
To listen to the silence,
Then onwards,
Jogging,
Laughter and clapping hands,
Railroads ahead

116 *Platform*

Through the railings,
Beyond the rail-track,
People pass and cars sail by
Like blancmanges,
Maddened by the slowness of Sunday
Raindrops peeling away from the surface
Of the lime-trees and rusted brick,
Leave them varnished
As the stones, that lie in beaded heaps
Around the lamp-posts.
A train approaches,
Splits the dampness,
Snake approaching,
Scatters the leaves and iron and rooftops
Into a thousand screaming jewels
That grow orange beneath the penetrating smoke.

117   *The Fainting*

When the pain comes,
Gold spots upon the darkening curve
Of a new world,
The people all around
Jingle up and down and smile,
Doe-faced, gentle-eyed.
Wearing soft fabric clothes
According to the latest fashion;
While wrapped in bands of steel,
Blood and flesh swirl
To win the fight,
Pulling down the knees to jellied nausea;
Lost upon a cloud of will-power,
Only ten seconds until the train will stop
Graciously before a wooden bench,
There to stay the pain
Awhile against the dew thickening into night,
Rustling with passengers around the kiosk
And up the steps;
Leaves and cloud console,
Until there is focus once more into relief;
Humdrum to lose that other curved earth
Of flesh and blood and bone,
Septic and aching,
Melted away.
Watching from afar
The lighted faces revolve,
Red-lipped, clownish.

118   *Party Time*

The party was a slit of light under the door
A glazed falsehood,
Piercing the circular eyes, peeling away the candlelight,
Sparks and shocks
To blot out the night
And join the guests together
In receding effervescence
Until all bubbles exploded
And it grew dark,
Time for the nightly ghosts to begin their uneasy prowl.

119 *Party Games*

Party games are fun.
Let's throw away all inhibitions.
You take off your tie and I'll take off my shoes
And we'll sit opposite each other
On the orange carpet, soft tuffs ruffled,
And tell each other a secret,
Something we have never told anyone else before, ever.
How strange to keep a secret bottled up all this time.
Effervescence released in surprise.
Perhaps you will despise me and I will condemn you.
No, we reassure each other of party loyalty,
Bound together by the yellow light
And the black fingers of shadows on the wall.
Your eyes are large and grey, fathomless contradictions.
You tell me that you are not normally candid
Not even to yourself,
But keep your thoughts hidden in greyness,
Grey as your eyes and your reticence.
I am always honest, so this little game
Is no novelty for me.
We laugh and link hands.
A shadow on the wall
Reminds us that this is eleven o'clock.
It is night. Yellow light flickers.

Now on a Friday morning
Traces of dust on our faces,
Searing white light illumines
And magnifies all blemishes,
We walk from opposite ends of the cold street,
Eyes cast down,
Locked in our different compartment of thought,
We do not see each other at first.
But as we pass, our eyelids flicker for a moment
In distasteful recognition.
The day is too white for subtleties,
Too cold for shadows released by the sun.
Only the naked outlines of the shop fronts
And two people in a deserted street,
Perplexed by the scorching white light of the day,
Which mocks them for thinking
That party games are fun.

120   *Dream of Oxford*

Is it a nightmare or a dream?
I see against a black sky a towering block of bedrooms,
Patched with yellow squares of light.
Through the window-panes students crouch
Over half-finished essays,
Long dressing-gowns, black shadow silhouettes.
The yellow squares pull me back, back into the past.
The rustle of essay notes;
Fingers piling together heaps of paper,
Cunning manipulation.
There is the silence of jumping minds at midnight,
A forest of tiny words scribbled and never read again,
A buzzing of love-affairs dissected and later forgotten.
The weight of their united adolescence reaches out
To touch the sky,
But instead squeezes my ventricles, churning black gloves
And the three o'clock dream fizzles out
Into yellow sparks,
Leaving only blackness.

121 *Christmas Eve*

After the cinema,
The painted eyes and candy-wrappers,
The pavement smacked up hard and jerky,
Line after line, a patchwork quilt upon the stone,
Each cross was a complete integrity
Of right angles, stretched out endlessly
As the wind blew cold in a parallel track
And wave upon wave of acceptance
Flowed down the street.
No enmity or duality was there,
But all was swept up into a hammock of this moment,
Which will always be somewhere,
To be prised out hour after hour
And retrieved in a blink of the eyelid,
Cast down towards the brown air of the evening.

Christmas Eve,
Yellow flames upon the stove,
Yellow flames of power,
Light rising from the black hub,
The black nest, where it all began.
Some cradle I see in the criss-cross of metal,
The heat is all there is,
The love that sweats and burns but will not burn out;
Can destroy only sometimes,
But leads onwards into the mess, the pulling depths.
The chewing flames twist out of the black air
Into the aura of birth.

122 *Reality*

A hidden chink,
Vulnerable
When the tide is out. The sea has ebbed
Far, far away along the stretches of white sand,
Leaving a row of naked footmarks,
A rubber balloon and an old tin can,
A heap of ordure,
The sleeve of a muddy shirt buried beneath the sand.
My faults exposed,
I can only stare at the dazzling whiteness
And wait for the tide to roll back,
Grey feathers upon white lace, the foam.
Once more protected,
I can forget the shock of this moment
And sleep
Until the next time.

PART VI

INDOORS

123 *Yoga*

After the visitors departed,
Slowly from the sofas in the sitting-room,
I cleared a space on the carpet
And began to stretch.
As arms reached high above head,
Muscles and tendons elongated,
From skull to toe,
I became a vertical line
And the earth that was grounded in my feet
Wanted to reach out
Above the distempered ceiling
To the black moth-eaten blanket of sky
That hung above
With no pretence.

124 *Mouse*

The mouse, a tiny grey ball of fur,
Has fallen asleep over its poisonous meal,
Is awoken by a pinch of rubber-gloved fingers,
Which fling it into the nearest wastepaper bin,
Yet gently, without crushing the little beast,
Moved perhaps by the tiny momentary squeak,
Which turns it into a child's plaything,
And thus demands courtesy.

125 *Insect*

The daddy long legs
Cannot scuttle quickly enough out of the primrose bath,
But confused by the artistry of modern plumbing,
Slithers up and down the shiny slopes,
A Nazi exercise.
The flailing legs dance a black wire can-can,
Half an inch above the steaming water's top.
I dredge from somewhere something of compassion
And slip a cool flannel beneath the whirring body.
It leaps onto the floor to find the reassurance
Of black and white squares,
As they fall into their familiar pattern of symmetry.
The wheeling legs slow down to a frozen hunch,
As I break through the barriers of four limbs
To the bafflement of a tiny, pointed world.

126 *Television*

Oh black and white machine of information,
Highly distracting to my concentration.
The book I read seems cold and full of lies,
While you are slyly mobile before my eyes.
I know you as a being one degree
Below the robot in the eternal hierarchy.
A robot can respond, but has no heart,
But you ignore me manacled to your art.
If only you were fruitful all the time
And I am not demanding the sublime,
But would prefer your noise to educate me,
Instead you jingle loud and irritate me;
For all too often you syncopate and crash
With what I shall entitle popular trash,
With violence and sex and ghastly comedy,
But since it's in demand, what is the remedy?
Instead I try to read without success,
For you are there to mock at me *sans cesse,*

127 *Reminder*

Sunday television, an Italian wartime movie,
The ranting mother, savage cheekbones,
And the raped daughter, eyes
Deranged by shock, pupils upturned.
I would like to upturn the volume louder and louder,
Until the metallic tubes and plastic knobs
Have fizzled out into an orange whirls of sparks,
Blue hiss of smoke,
Annihilating the droning tanks,
The square-shouldered satin evening gowns,
And the old women, black bundles,
Nodding to themselves.
They live on in miniature in the colour supplements,
Framed with suitable captions,
But the twenty-three-inch face
That speaks to me on the screen,
Pupils gazing into mine,
Is an intrusion.

128 *Passive Involvement*

Try to absorb
The news on television
Of a flood, a murder, a railway crash.
In my armchair,
Legs splayed and fingers sagging into torpor,
Slippers on the carpet spring up from time to time
With the resilient push of the woollen tufts.
To bear vicarious pain at all times
Is difficult.
A continual participation
In the throbbing line of people
Linked together problematically
Like a reel of cotton knotted at intervals.
The points are small, almost invisible.
Only the finger probing with careful thought
These networks of thread.
Not easy. Deliberate patience.
Effort of passive involvement.

129   *The Deaf Ear*

The pounding Beethoven,
Beats crotchets upon the beige carpet of the bedsitter.
And the girl shrieks above the waves of his lament
Into the mouth of the telephone,
Hearing neither the voice at the other end, suburbs away,
Nor the pleas of the composer a century ago,
Yet equally demanding.

130 *The Search*

Perhaps this daily journal,
Pages of red ink, words dwindling to horizontal scribble,
Each day marking a new encounter,
Perhaps this self-indulgence should not be allowed
By my better judgment,
But the finished notebook,
Flopping from the weight of total honesty,
The cast-off skin of my growing self,
Gives food to nourish the inner core of my being.

131   *Why Write?*

I wrote away at ease until the poets
Acquainted me with their new sophistication.
Unnerved and shattered by their subtle breadth,
I recognised with awe their cool finesse.
Why write, I thought, when what I write is limited
To the delicacy of a narrow woman's attitude?
I am not well acquainted with their jargon,
Nor can I jingle wittily and dirtily,
With illusions to the sensational and the bizarre,
But then with resignation I soon determined
To follow up my own particular pattern,
Resolve my individual themes and questions,
Well limited perhaps but still defined:
An accurate survey of a single mind.

132   *The Poet*

The poet looks   out
Of his head
Sieves   and
Synchronises experience
Catches here   a silver ball
And there   an eyelash sliver
Of upside down images.
His friend helps quiet a lot
With new catchy phrases
And the strong sally
Of criticism.
The poet is
Sometimes
Very happy   to think
New   verses
But mostly impatient
Waiting
Waiting   for it
To happen
Next.

133   *To Write*

His writing is more real to him than life.
It forms the daily marrow.
External details merely husk and skin.
Cushioned by the knowledge of this mechanism in him,
Which converts all pain to words, he lives
A false pleasure and smiles.

She writes sporadically to define the stabs
That cannot be resolved,
By others, perhaps, but not by her.
She suffers. But his grimace is worse.

134 *Writing*

After a long gap between poem
And poem
Invention strikes the automatic pen
As a bonus, a skill, devised to produce fancy words
Like an icing set tricked out by deft fingers.
These phrases bear no relation to the surprised author,
Who reads through the legible output
With the embarrassed scrutiny
Of a close relative.

PART VII

THE TEN DAYS OF PENITENCE

135 *The Ten Days of Penitence*

Slowly the evil
Has seeped into my soul.
Rusted.
I cannot feel an assurance,
That all is burnt out in the boiling
Of time,
But feel the rot.
I am no longer myself,
But a black shape
Against the shades of a water-mauve sky
In the middle of a swarm of black shapes,
Waiting
For the reckoning.

136 *Memory*

A frightening thing is memory,
Sometimes it has such intensity.
A moment of insight sparks up alive
And illumines the present with brevity.
But soon the glow is fully erased
And the mind is an empty black slate again.
Often when defects are overcome
And promises made and hates discarded,
We find that the following intricate day
Involves such triviality
That the spark is nearly obliterated,
Devoured by the fangs of petty routine,
Return and glow, each moment of worth
With kaleidoscopic density
To nourish and fill the continual need
Of my inner thirsting immensity,
And form a flashing, active will
Wherever I may breathe or be.

137 *Egg*

I am an egg.
A black band in the middle separates
The lower brown cup from the upper white.
Down below, the turbulence of the idd
Rages against the white shell of the superego
And they meet together in the black band,
The judo belt of the creative impulse.

138   *Roaming*

Pain produces logic
To anaesthetise
By justification;
What if this jumbled scream
Were nothing more
Than that,
A screaming jungle,
To roam among triangular leaves long hours
And never to find the hypotenuse?

139 *Filter*

Without the selectivity
Of a brain filter,
All experience flames upon the ground
Meaningless, chaotic,
An LSD trip misfired.
And so, with little finger elevated
I make a fastidious choice
And remain coherent.

140 *Brain*

Sharpen the brain
To a fine point of precision,
So that it sizzles with electricity
And in the coils of red glow
Insights will emerge
From the dazzle of unleashed thoughts.

141 *Jealousy*

The green eyes of the black tomcat stare into mine,
As I pour a carton of cream into a lopsided pan,
Flickering deprivation of white I possess
By right of human dominance,
Which gives me ten fingers of bone
And a brain to obtain what is mine.
The black ovals upon emerald criss-crossed eyes
Wane with my pain of human complexity.

142 *Distrust*

Cannot trust you,
Though know you well.
Feel your duality,
Dichotomy of love.
Wish you well,
But put my own interests before yours
And well you know it,
So you give back nothing,
And I cannot trust you,
Distancing you through
The picture-frame stage of observation.

143 *The Scapegoat's Cry*

A guilt I feel, which is not needed, yet wanted.
A punishment I know, which I long to suffer.
Their mindless cruelty pleases me though hurtful
And simpers like a friend, wanting to please me
For pain grows pure in nervous self-defence
And soon I start to love the thrill of cruelty,
The bully's bow that fears to face his equals.
I love the lashing wildness of his anger
Which bears me up to face humiliation
I thrill with pain as order, calm and neutral
Returns to numb my ache in recompense.

144 *The Choice*

You saved my life with your rock love.
Steadfast gaze, pillar of ice,
That would not let me sink into the helter-skelter,
But drew me into your own shadow-cave of knowing.
Long ago, it seems, I declined the blackness of giving all
For the yellow butter sunlight, godless laughter,
And when a moment ago I looked into your tranquil eyes,
And saw hazel waters moving, smiling, waiting,
I regretted my refusal.

145 *Display*

The person who knows you well –
The knowledge may be fractional,
But you do not know the fraction –
Cannot be avoided, evaded.
So you must submit to the godlike nod,
That slowly mesmerises,
The subtle lowering of the voice,
That reminds you of your telepathic bondage.
And when you try to camouflage
An x-ray effort shoots out, a green flame
To see behind your ploys,
So you can only accept,
And walk around naked,
Hideous, but unashamed.

146 *Questions and Answers*

'It is rude,' said Alice, 'to make personal remarks.'
The boy with the deerlike face asks the woman,
'Where do you work?' and shrivels away, as she frowns
Pebble-eyed back. 'Why do you want to know?'
No reason explicable, but the age-old wish
To communicate.
She reads between the lines and pours out
Eye-pools of acid onto his frightened scrutiny.
Across the room a girl laughs between ropes of black hair
And shouts, 'I work in Islington.'

If only I knew the answer, the answer,
If I could crack the mirror into a thousand splinters,
If I could reach through to the other side
Like Alice, but what answer did she find?
A fairytale entertainment.
The image I see is an overlapping duet,
The retina trick of a drunkard on a spree,
The white and the black, the knowing and the searching.
Only a glass, a pure glass, can give the answer,
No dust on the frozen surface,
No silvered gleam to distract from the true reflection.
I will throw a diamond rose through the mirror
Into the black night sky, Through the dust particles
Beyond the magnetic sphere of this constellation
And the splintered petals will tinkle a frozen answer.

147 *The Will*

The essence of goodness,
However multiplex one's faults,
Is to rise above
And in losing selfness to become godlike,
A non-person.
Breath exhaled on a snowy day
Cannot be concealed, but puffs out white clouds,
Ghostly against the damp air.
The pressure of the will will out
And away from a bone-house too small,
Will burst from the shrinking body.

148 *Instant*

When the pain rings true,
Like charnel-fire through the body of a snake,
There is the bliss of waiting
For cessation.

149   *God and Satan*

Satan grew so bright
That he sparked out.
God hangs darkly.
Satan whistled a sibilant hiss,
That pierced through to another world.
God is immobile everywhere.
Satan loves and links
With gold rings in a chain of paper-foil,
That slithers apart.
God clamps even polarities together
In a pressure-hold.
That is what
He is.

150 *Psychology*

We live in the age of psychology,
Where quiet and willpower
Have vanished as true qualities,
And have been reabsorbed into the sea of pathology,
Where love and hate may be controlled by biochemistry,
Where sleep and waking
Are merely different manifestations
Of the ego lulled into various states of awareness,
Where God is a conglomeration
Of all the medieval manuals,
Bound together into one neat conformity,
Where the norm is elevated to an abnormal degree
And the abnorm is compressed into mediocrity.
No , I am not mocking,
Not baiting,
Not hating,
Just stating,
And waiting,
To see what further advances are in the making.

151 *Sanity*

Sanity lies in emotional wholeness.
The maniac's mind may be vital and probing
But his feelings are over-developed, so dangerous
To himself and his neighbours and all the community.
A well-ticking intellect with fickle stability,
He speaks to his visitor open and friendly,
With rational meaning and sensible calmness.
An instant's meandering starts up the curtain
Dividing the insane from the sane majority.
His visitors' eyes blink, glaze and lose contact.
He's labelled and separated, alone and still thinking.

152 *The Future*

Unlike the gypsy in the tent with a glass ball
And a cup of tea-leaves,
I can never quite believe in the future.
My tent is the present moment,
Which cloaks out all things to come.
Trapped by the moist moment of each breath,
I do not see any shapes on the screen of the coming week,
And so I am bound by a caul of disbelief,
For as the days pass by, the birth-pangs of all new ideas
Stretch my vision until I want to shriek
With the agony of a future
That insists itself, despite my stolid denial.

153   *Evil*

Id,
Evil id,
Burning cantankerous in the fires of the self.
Where do I lie.
That chose to be?
Would sing and love and grow.
Down there
Bubbles black
Clotted blood, that is stirred to hatred.
Roots,
Clump into the night,
Where the soul knows
The one,
To whom it belongs,
Death trap of horned gold,
Leaping a grotesque comedy.
Rise
Out slowly finger above palm above hand
And shriek free.

154 *Turbulence*

Cannot find peace of mind,
Blue sky haven,
In the turbulence of craggy stone-sifted quarry,
Black coals crunching over sparkled flints
Cannot find peace.
Only the rough shifting of not knowing,
The ache of the changing motions of the rocks,
As they churn together this way and that,
Granulated squeaks,
Cannot find peace.

155 *Façade*

She wants to be happy.
Her voice is frosted white lace upon a rose glass,
And when a disturbance arises,
Monstrous spider, black against the window-pane.
She freezes its wiry legs
And watches the mouldy remains,
That rot away far on into the winter.

156 *Current of Belief*

Tired of pure thoughts, crisp, snowflake white,
I switched off the current of belief in God
And waited to see what would happen.
Driven along by my own motor-power,
Curious movements, often wires intermingled,
Spirits of energy bouncing along the ground,
Evolved from my fear and hatred.
Magnet removed, I experienced
A chaos.
Switched on the electricity again,
Crossed wires slip back to normal.
Peace of mind, perhaps, but not quite,
Having once glimpsed behind the fence.

157 *Double Glazing*

You think you made a precise and unusual discovery,
That everybody has a façade, a double-glazing.
Smash away this outer layer and expose the inner glass.
You behave this way with everybody,
Undiscriminating,
Exposing your unhappiness, your fears.
But I consider this continual vandalism
To be even falser than the double barrier
That preceded it.
Leaves no room for layers to be gradually pared away,
Like the peeling of an onion,
Which makes one cry genuine tears,
Not the coal moan of affectation.

158 *The Line of Memory*

Keats wrote somewhere
That when two old friends meet
After a lapse of seven years,
They will be totally changed in every tissue.
I have seen this happen,
Watched them gaze at each other curiously,
Newly estranged,
But drawn together by the line of memory
They each pull out of their minds an image of the past
And dangle it on a string, smiling bashfully.
I would like to label all these images
And place them in a universal library
For the reference of future generations,
But this can never be.
Meanwhile people will write plays and paint pictures
To rid themselves of the ache of old memories,
Which clutter up their minds, swollen to bursting point.
And in the expulsion a shrinking will take place
And a transfiguration.

159 *Over-Exposure*

Tightening threads break through
The churning heart-tissue.
My slow frown
I see for the first time
The face of the Jamaican girl or woman,
The label is inappropriate as is her race.
Fuzzy down of hair, extended nostrils,
Pushed by invisible rings from ear to ear,
She tries to smile,
Soft lips curiously knowing
The black and the white of every day.
Unblinking wet eyes, that stare into mine.
Encounter unfamiliar,
I turn away.

The cliff-face is white from over-exposure.
It is a free choice
To outstare all that is wrong
And see only the blotted remains
Or to feel with the snails crushed into the cliffside.
When the rocks grow to sand, and the seaweed to slime,
All is broken in the floodwaters,
Even the black and white films,
Spotted from over-exposure
Show skeleton figures bent towards the prison camps

Quick march of flashing teeth as the snakes flow in
Onto semi-corpses.
Everyone is black and white and spotted.
To stare through their smiles
Beyond their knowing
And to share the corpse
That they will one day be
Is a free choice,
A choice that is right
Or to let every exposure grow blind and white.

160 *Rat-Race*

Rat-race,
Squeaks in the running.
Leap over a grey back and a brown back.
Prick up your ears twitching to catch some gossip.
Destroy his reputation, her peace of mind.
Run as far as you can over the dead leaves,
For nothing can survive in this climate.
Knife of wind over the runway,
Gasping for breath,
Tiny pointed teeth peep out of sagging mouth,
Surprise of red blood
Pouring out from beneath the grey fur,
A reminder that it is still alive but not for long,
Squeaks in the bleeding.
Rat-race.

161 *Reflector*

You are a non-person.
You do not have thoughts of your own,
Only echo mine and embroider.
In your eyes, small and deep-set grey,
I see myself reflected, minimised.
You write about me as though I were not a person,
But an image,
To pin inside a compartment of your mind,
Made for the purpose of categorisation,
My eccentricities defined
And gummed down for ever
Onto paper.
A photographic lens that captures
With a trick of light.
Clever gimmicks.
After my life's and I will be immortalised
By your skill.
Favour
That I do nor relish.

162 *Tightrope*

A tightrope of people.
Every word must be weighed and measured.
Be careful how you tread.
Each figure walks stiffly enclosed
In his own tube of ice.
Do not breathe too warmly
Or the coating will melt,
A painful thaw,
To swell and to ache,
Exposing
Collapsible limbs.
The bodies will fall off the tightrope screaming.
Hold in your breath and the rigid figures
Will continue to advance their zombie walk.

163 *Eyes*

Five different faculties have we unknowing.
Only tired eyes,
Hot glass,
Crossed lashes,
Remind us.
Four and a half left, we see the world through a barrier,
Conscious for the first time of our separation
From the space around us.
Individual outline defined by helplessness,
We grope in the dark,
Throbbing eyelids, sore skin, ounce of flesh so valuable
Cannot be denied.
Network of red lines spidery in the white iris,
Pink worms in a jelly of milk,
Opaquely
We try to see.

164 *Success*

Problems, that litter the mind like pebbles on a beach,
Grey, large and shiny.
A Nazi task to carry a bucketful up a hill
And throw them down again.
Unending cascade.
Select a few fossils and weed out a shoalful
Of stones, clink upon the sand.
Only by sifting can we see
The pattern of a past Palaeolithic age,
Losing our integrate
In the determination to survive.

165 *Oyster*

Silently, as the days pass,
We wait for the scratch, the irritation
From which to nourish our thoughts, poems growing,
Like the pearl inside an oyster, swelling day by day
From the grain of sand within.
Ironically, no happiness is possible, or very rare.
For undisturbed by thought, we find a grotesque vacuum,
And so we wait with perverse logic,
For the pinch, the scratch
And enjoy the septic swelling.

166　The Smile

The smile,
A long-remembered habit,
Cannot be changed by practice or artifice.
Forty years in an office, her guarded words, quick coughs
And the smile peeps out
From three years old.
Eight teeth beneath the stretched upper lip.
Almost a rabbit, saved by pearly equality.
Naked to the white airlight
The teeth gleam and disappear
Behind the filing system.

The mother, brown arms, goose-pimples,
Magnolia perfume, wipes the soap-suds off her fingers
And onto her apron.
She smiles into the pram,
Closed lips, her teeth cloaked into oblivion,
Along with her own solitary childhood.

167 *Needlepoint*

Through a forest of taboos and ill-fortune
Love winds its devious path,
To strike a heart with the prick of a needle.
The valve is punctured,
Bubbles over into death,
Black blood, to be reborn
A different person, one skin less,
Open to a multitude
Of new and finer pricks.

168   Four-Leaved

People
Cluster like clover in the meadows,
One solitary flower by the fence
And here a four-leaved gem,
Arousing admiration and perplexity;
It stabs at so-called normality.
Boundaries divide people,
A delicate membrane here,
And here a skin, a hide, a barrier,
To break the partitions
Is frowned upon.
Only the four-leaved oddity can indulge, succeed
Unpunished.

169 *Two Cures*

The Stoic
Thickens his skin with oil and will-power
Not to feel.
Fortified
By the precaution that all is pain
He grins hugely.

The poet
Scrapes off the outer surface of his skin,
Bare cellulose.
It bleeds differently every day.
The fun of exploration.
Sometimes the flesh is raw.
He weeps with his wound,
But soon recovers defiantly.

170   *Two Sides*

A phone-call from a woman
Who was my rival twelve years ago,
As we sat in his room side by side on a sofa,
Olive-green silk with faded threads of white.
I noticed the black hairs upon her neck,
Her short neck
Set at anxious angle.
The squeak in her voice,
A restlessness probing but never profound.
She stirred my envy.
I watched gloatingly
As she curved a wrist against her chin,
Ugly
In a false attempt to allure.
Now she is a mother.
I feel ashamed. Her attempt was not false,
Yet neither was my vision incorrect.
Both sides of the triangle are just.
They fall from the apex, which is herself
Onto the hypotenuse of perception,
Reflected in the sight of her lover and myself
Today and yesterday.

171 *Involvement*

Hypocritical
With each change of department,
Faction and political party,
We laugh behind your back,
Your retreating figure harmless,
Black suit shrinking into the distance,
We smile unthinking. Not wise to probe too deep.
Compromise in order to survive.
Only when suddenly you swivel round,
Eyes narrowed to angry slits,
Your mouth open in surprise,
Upper lip curved back in disrespect,
A keyboard of white teeth flashing.
Comes realisation.
Lurching heartbeat.
Guilt.

172 *Divorce*

After all this time
Only a brick wall left.
Your head has banged against it uselessly
All these years.
It has not grown any softer.
No indentations to rest upon,
No mossy patches for the cushioning.
You have tried again and again to reach him.
No shadows left to darken the bricks, crudely pink.
The wall stands bolt upright in the naked sunlight
A barrier between you,
And now you must crawl away into the background,
Acknowledging your mistake.

173 *Widow Spider*

They spoke blunt friendship
And their words murdered each other;
Like a female spider
That devours its mate,
She surveyed the void where he
No longer existed,
But snarled feebly, defeated,
Until the next silence should lasso them
Into a frozen circle.

174 *Sophistication*

Warm, friendly voice,
Cultivated adjustment to individuality,
She talks at ease to everyone,
Caring for none.
Gimmicks, trick gestures, here a raised eyebrow,
There a lifted arm, head turned to the side,
Twitch of cheeks, strained nod,
Eyes understanding.
Blue pupils naked upon the white iris,
Joined to every glance in total comprehension
And complete indifference.

175 *Photo*

Now that you are thirty
You have recaptured the features
Of your childhood, sturdy obstinacy,
Little-boy petulance.
The downcast face to retreat into the corner and sulk.
In the intervening years of adolescence,
When you really grew up,
You were defiant and rebellious, a man upstanding.
But now you have shrunk back into your old shadow,
The hand slipping into the right glove,
A comfortable habit.
I cannot blame you. Perfectly natural to retrieve
The proper image.
But I miss the shiny negative.

176 *Fifty Per Cent*

Can you not accept the fact
That I can only love you fifty per cent?
The remainder is taken up with jealousy.
I am a half and half person,
And I do not wish to change.
So if you want a hundred per cent dotage
Do not come to me.
Or perhaps the others are just as fractional as myself,
But conceal it.
They play tricks on you,
Whereas my duplicity is naked.
Thus in all logic
You must accept my calculated honesty
And love me with whatever degree of fervour
Seems appropriate.

177   *No Resting Place*

Now
No love is here
To you
Rolled back into the black ether,
Your own self
Where you belong.
Long ago
I found a surprise,
Summer growing,
Green upon green,
Touched me.
And ever the humming grows louder,
Where there is no end
To the one creation.
New weeds will grow apace
Yellow furze, brown bushes,
The sickening turning over
Lurches back into Sartoris' opened eye.
There is no resting place,
I want to cry.

178 *Infection*

Infection
Takes us out of the cardboard paint
Into an underworld,
Where the body bubbles black and sick,
Spawning with some knife-stab
To grow whole again.
Bubbles float along the air from the clay pipe,
Red streaks in the soap-silk skin
And the child blowing breath after breath,
Laughing at the slow flow.
Blood and germs mingle and fight within the body
And the owner continues to advance,
Pinned down momentarily
By black bubbles of sickness.

179 *Wasted Years*

The wasted years
Thrown down a well,
Brown tidemarks swoop up high;
Can never be pulled back,
Dwindled to a sixpence of mud,
No frantic retrieval of every split second
Can fill in the white hairs of the empty days,
Before the act of decision clamped down
The expansion into adulthood.

180 *Acquiescence*

I accept this, the stifled past,
I can endure
With my acquiescence.
A tribute to those
Half-skeletons, the cramped angles of their lives.
I can redress the balance,
Annul my debit
To the forgotten surfs and mothers of fourteen
And deeds woven by archival convention;
The love that could never be given
And the strange tumbling down of days
One upon the other
In infantile confusion.

181 *Frost*

The half people,
Who live cramped days
Like tulips
Bitten by frost
Before the air has blown them out.
Will never know
The strange expanse.
Instead they breathe securely
The dead hours.

182 *Meditating*

All digging down to the same roots.
We reach the green
And wait.
Stopped
Upon a patch of cool,
The eye trapped
Into a glazed holding.
Wait here.
Minutes are nothing, not even hours.
We are here, here in the leaf-green grip.
Before and after is dancing,
But now
The static eye blinks, pupil glossy curve of blue
Mesmerised to a marble
Of water.
Deep down
To the point of a pool,
Grey and silver layers
Of probing.

183 *Six Haikus*

Peach row of faces
Frozen into scrutiny,
As words resolve pain.

The cat jumps up in delight
To lick the ice-cream plates,
While we wash up.

Beneath the wooden pier
The slits of sea gleam through,
Blue as April sky.

Around the boardroom table
Sit half a dozen men
In grim discourse.

Beyond the library hush
A piano clinks out chords,
Then fades away.

The silence presses down,
Willing me to speak
Or scream or shout or weep.

184   *Respect for the Elders*

Respect for the elders,
Is it a tyranny of the old over the young,
An ancient hierarchy gone wrong,
Or the growth of wisdom over the years
So that at the point of death
All is conceived in the upturned eye,
Roll of white egg?

The old page of the Bible
Has been torn out and crumpled away
Today,
So that only the jottings are left,
Shepherd on the hillside
Under the burning Middle Eastern sun
And another son bringing home
A smile of obedience
To the old parents still lodged
In his childhood home.

185 *Snowdrop*

I am one person.
Sometimes the snowdrop opens,
Key turns and the petals curve out.
To give
Sun meets the frostbitten fringe of brown tatters.
Only one person.
Stream of thought always alone,
Inside the white bird of head,
Flows out ice-cream clear on smooth days,
To lasso another
Merge
Then falls back into two twines.
One person alone
Has given you the full stream onslaught,
Ice-deep melting waves of lace
Into translucency
And now,
Frozen over by glass-case of winter,
Fall back again into the bird,
One person alone.

186 *The Ascetic*

Will eat
Only the bitter flesh of apple and lemon.
Live on rub of sparkle stones against the knuckles,
Cushions of shingle
To wear away the padded flesh;
Granulated winds will wash me clean.
Tear away the blood luxury
Into knives of bone
Skeleton,
Pearl white,
Purified hollow of cheeks,
Where the shadows reflect the old worn-out trunks
Of passing trees,
That have eaten their way into the ground
With roots of tentacle.

187 *War Baby*

Listening
To the hardy battleaxe
Anecdotal with pride
Behind the beige upholstery,
I changed from audience to participant
And lingered in the spiral of her voice-box,
Where children sobbed a full ten minutes
For their fathers,
Departed with the army;
Until at the last
I was a three-year-old girl
In rubber dungarees,
Playing
Anyhow
But never anywhere
In trouble

188   *Occupational Therapy*

Grey slabs that peel down
To neat shapes
Beneath manipulating fingers.
Soon the patients will leave
With new personalities,
The spare grey slabs discarded,
A gift to the memory of the word,
Just as Adam bestowed a spare rib to Eve
And watched the consequences grow.

189 *Camera*

You hate my barren mind
And long for the round green leaf bush
That trembles to every vibration of the wind
And grows fatter every year.
Yet I can only spread a white silence
That seeps into the world around me
And clarifies the images
Into a photographic portrait for ever.

190 *Sacrifice*

Do not be dependent upon the one
Whom you would wish to lean upon,
But keep yourself free
The black nugget of identity.
A wheel with gold sparks spinning and flashing
Will revolve day by day,
Catching new loves within its circle
And forking away
The old road,
Until one day
Concentrated thought, drops of selfhood,
Will knit you together with the outer world
And you will both be reunited
With the surprised smile of a bonus
That had been willing to be sacrificed.

191 *Fallen Away*

There was the first man
And the first woman
The others fell away
Replicas of the father and the mother,
And the earth began to crumble
When the flowers grew,
Tiny images that sprang up,
New and rubbery into the surprised air.
We are all fallen away
From the dead hanging air,
The hard outline of wood and steel and aluminium
Into the gift of present vision.

192 *Song of the Crow*

Inside my head
Fly
A white bird and a black bird
The white bird unrolls a sheet of lace before my eyes
And sings of peace;
The black bird croaks that I am no better than the rest
To stand one day amidst the rows of bodies,
Dead pillars of white chalk
And share the final writing upon the wall.
The white bird hands me gifts,
Nuggets of gold
And watches the hours fly across.
Swollen into bubbles;
They burst and pass below.
The black bird stares,
Eyes buttoned into tight reproach,
And crows
The living moment.

193   *We Follow Our Gods*

We follow our gods
Doggedly,
Making of them what we will;
Unmaking
Those that bend
And refuse to torment.
Those strange sunglassed hours
When everybody loves
Everybody,
A cavernous insistence
Still beats the humdrum timpani of hatred;
And a whirring of lorry-wheels
As
Back
Down
The well
They grow dumb
Shoe-steps forwards
Will find along the dust
A new flight of dust.

194 *Fire*

You turn your loves into gods,
Pillars to lean upon,
White fire
Along the day
Hover.
These ghosts of strength,
Sad-eyed,
Willing,
But unable to open the eye
Of the window
Which cuts the sky
Into white fire.

Strength of you,
Crag of shoulders,
Wedge of eyes,
Scrutinise.
You spindle a thread,
Straight as the crow flies,
Truthful,
While the silhouettes around you
Sharpen in surprise
And the window
Cuts the sky
Into white fire.

195 *Tulip*

Fixed
Upon a tulip,
I saw
Blue tinged upon pink,
Like lips in winter;
Severe
Drew the centre
Of whirling Saturday
Down,
Compressed
To the growing point.
Where static
Lies the root of
His pain
And mine,
To whirl endlessly,
Mocked by angels upon a pin,
Who enjoy
What they can understand,
Which we shall never know.

196 *Smiled Upon a Face*

Smiled upon a face
That offered nothing in return.
Eyes brown stones.
Caverned into the skeleton,
Where the flesh receded
And grew saggy,
A death's head,
Lumbering down the corridor,
Pulling back to old arches of cloisters
And grey places,
That fizzled into silence
Before they started the coil
Of turbulent vision.

197 *Cycle*

Leaves crush branches,
Emerald sting of spices;
Stones edged with corners press into worms
And splinter the red tongues of jelly.
Sky upon skull upon heel
Weigh down
To this larva cycle of
The spinning earth.
Cannot stop,
Caught up
In the onslaught.
Cruel to crush,
But no schism
Can separate the stones away from the earth;
Bodies that float into a long airshaft
Will fall, decay.
Compressed
Is this wheel,
Spinning,
Cohesive,
To gravity.

Germs,
Yellow grubs,
Beads on a string,

Tell a rosary
Of all the diseases
That grow.
This body is a myth:
Four sausages stuck to a lollipop.
The head grins.
A keyboard of teeth
Play a tune
On the xylophone
Plaintive clink,
Like dripping water,
Knows it will fall
Into a whirlpool
Of decay,
Disintegrate
Beneath the fresh earth.
The soil is good and moist
Enough to thrust up snails and larvae.
Beneath the sky,
Wind blows a sail of sweeping Wedgwood
On a hot day,
Burnt into the blue.
The Earth is quiet enough to hear itself ticking
As it remembers all the bodies it holds
In the grip of love.
Vacantly the sphere
Revolves
In the blink of an eye.

The old man sleeps
In the launderette,
Slumped upon a settee of pure alcohol
He wheezes to catch his breath;
An air bubble, caught somewhere
In the red plantwork of his ventricles,
Emits a thin whistle.
If only the knotted organ would
Swell in and out again,
Like the syncopated glove it used to be,
The washing behind the convex glass
Dangles one way and then the other.
Caught in a hiccup,
It cannot complete the cycle
While the sleeper, bent into the chest
Of his brown raincoat,
Dreams of the earth spinning around on its axis
Until the sky and sea all tumble back
Over the green fields
Through the black pathways
Of the night.

A cycle of futility and decay,
As birds fly, wings flutter downwards,
Turn to grey soot;
Each morning the alarm-clock bell rings in dismay
To find itself trapped again
In that 24-hour game of chance.
And people smile.
Disembodied Cheshire cat grins,

Which stay in the memory
Long after the happy day,
And everything that crumbles
Learns once again to cohere
In that cycle of futility and decay.

Everyone must be broken at the wheel.
Turn around
At the centre of all things,
There lies a beating heart
That signals the rhythm
Between the cracks of the pavements
And the twigs on the branches.
The cars that press along the road
In time to the stamp and grip
Of wheels against the ground
And a fantail of birds that splay across the sky
Grains against the blue,
Swimming helplessly.
The love between us all wheels into hatred
And back to love again
Carelessly,
Yet generous with the easy tumble forwards
Of the pulse
That tells the day and night.

198 *Sun on the Track*

Sun on the track,
Three rods of fire,
Slipping endlessly along the crushed field of stones.
The parallels change,
The bars intersect
Like a film out of sequence.
The journey goes on,
Goes on.

199 *No Further Can I Go*

No further can I go surely
Than to sink
To the centre of the earth,
Where churning lava performs its cycle daily,
Burnt out to ashes.
In that split second,
When metallic sky closes against the ground,
Is a shattering.
Air vibrates and surfaces are frozen into
Bare solidity.

200 *Wallflower*

Out of the barren mind
Flew
A wallflower,
The last to dance
And the first to arise
Into surprised life,
Grew
Flustering and wounded
By the strange winds,
That cut in sharp contradiction
And persisted.
Its cloying perfume
Will endure
Always.

201 *Peace*

Slowly
Unfolds
White salt peace,
Falling
Away from the action of silence
Into my shadow
That layers the floor with dust.
Half good,
Half thinking wind it clings.
The cutting off would be
A death.
I can look this moment straight
And fly to the bull's eye,
All around the circles grow larger and larger
Spreading out into the world
Of traffic and sky and tower-blocks,
Concrete and glass windows.
Tiny figures walking down the streets
Between crevices of buildings.
Here on high, I can watch the ants march by,
Slowly
Unfolds
White salt peace,
Falling
Away from the action of silence
Into my shadow.

Before and After
the Darkness

There at the centre
All other objects dropped
Now
Frozen
Into a realisation of what has been lost
The curves and angles shudder
Between before and after
Swing into focus.

from *Between Before and After*

If I could help you along the way, my love
I would do so willingly
But there is too much work to be done
For one person or even two or three
Too much darkness to be swept away
Darkness and shadows
Equivocal and obscure.

from *Before and After the Darkness*

This world is topsy-turvy
There is no cause for blame.

from *Topsy Turvy*

1   *Winter Dampness*

Winter dampness is a fungus
Time to rehearse one's shortcomings
The metallic sky rings guilt
Toast and oranges by the kitchen stove
Are an artifice
To hide the shivering afternoon
Out of doors the pavement clinks into bruises
The double glazing of the shopping parade
Is numb with furniture and lampshades
Comforts that are cleared away
By the blind silver light

2   *Reality Smiles*

Reality smiles,
Does not grow any happier
Though it repeats the pattern daily.
Two facing mirrors reflect forever
Into a tunnel of glass arches
Clear as cold liquid
Seeking
I find sometimes a new place
Invisible
Rippled.

3   *Whale Ideas*

Whale ideas
Blubber home
We press on
Further to find
New reflections
In the lashes of mud-water
That sink into us
We are fish
And fish blubber
And see island
And dry land is not sea
A long way ahead
Filters
Flesh through the network
One day
We will look at the rising sun
Gold sparks above the sea
Nearly forgotten
Now pierced
By the surprised eye
Which sees
The heat against the liquid
Gold as memory
Flesh the light of the sun like oil
On the curious wetness
Of penetrated water.

4   *The Past*

Canniballed
Not aware
I have absorbed them
Into my first
They multiply
Like worms
That make the calm good
Tell old stars in eyes
That grew angels
Every one of them
I will keep
Revolving
Will not let dissolve
The memory
Never throw back
To an old happening

5   *Through the Needle's Eye*

In me
You stay
White fire
Along the day
Spindle the thread
Through the needle's eye
Point flashes cold and then hot
Through the peach of the skin
Always I see the dark
A sky, growing old
And eyes
Seeing

6 *Honesty*

Strength of you
Crag of shoulders
Wedge of eyes
Scrutinise
Straight as the crow flies
Truthful
Where the silhouettes around you
Sharpen in surprise
And the window cuts the sky
Into fire

7 *Something Is Lost*

Crack
Between dawn and morning
The curtains half shut onto a grey sky
Something is lost, broken
In the hanging air.
The stove is grimed with rings of food
Crisped against the enamel
Pounding in my head
The face of a man
Resentful
Stirs out of my grasp
Lurches away
The carpet has knobs on
The clock ticks.

8   *Luck*

A gratuitous gift
A letter of good fortune flutters to the mat
I read it uneasily
Strange twist of normal combat to win
The bubble in my head swelling to a globe
And thoughts drift unconnected in the vacuum
Cannot enjoy the winning
The success
Separates me from living.

9   *Saturday Night*

Saturday night
The broken down fire
Fuses the flat
Into an older winter
Red flares across the snow
As the moon treads heavily
Soon the wolves will sing and howl
The curves of ice will sweep across the earth
The hulk of sky and mountaintops
Will spin in sleep
No-one cares
Alone
The sleeping bodies
Wait
For the whine to abate
And roast back into black comfort
Breathing like metronomes
To balance
The terror
Out there

10   Frightened of the Night

I am frightened of the night
That suckers the room
Into a standing pool
Where cars scream in the distance
A shaft of light blows an oblong ghost
Onto the painting on the wall
Around the bed
Hang old misdeeds
Pincered like crabs
That will punish me
I am frightened of the night
That suckers the room
Into a standing pool

11 *Dreams Talk*

She slept in a chair by the table
At her side of the room
While we talked with the windows open
And the wind rolled over her hair
It ruffled the black strands into clouds over her neck
And our talking crept into her dreams
Her peacefulness spread over us
It soothed us into silence
And her dreams began to talk out loud
And she spoke our conversation
The voice of her past life
The child that she had been spoke out
And spoke to the children in us
Rolling us back into her past
The open window ruffled
The waves of air, the dust on the floor
And past and present crashed
Into a drama of sleep.

12 *Blue*

Thinking is away from the grain
Of blue indolence
Needlepoints that flash hotly
Into staccato
The old man in the watch-shop
Has meshed
Amongst the pink chrome
Slowly totters up the bill
Alarm bells ring
Soon the blue sky will descend.

13 *Double Edged*

Love, once wanted,
Panacea to blunt all edges
And turn the pavements pink
Is not so
It is a knife into the heart
Where black and gold
Crack into shattering explosion
Frightens the eye away.

If I had loved one jot less
There would have been no self-murder
In this giving
If he had loved one jot less
There would have been no destruction
In my surrender.

14   *Fall*

Blighted
Earth waved return to its former crystal,
Eden blue and red and green,
Washed colours in the rain;
Feels the eagle
Hover over its cracks,
Split
Into trembling.
The wing-shafts whirr and hover;
Brain engulfment.

15 *Topsy-Turvy*

The criminal is ill,
Steals in surprise.
Stick arms in hospitals
Wait for sympathy
White as grapes
This world is topsy-turvy
There is no cause for blame.

16 *Two o'clock*

Net curtains quiver
Like loops of jelly
The gable opposite
Presses over windows
Peacock blue
Whistle and moan of traffic
Damp air floating to dispersal
This two o'clock is too peaceful
To be real

17   *Cracked Heart*

Heart cracked into jagged edges
Like a knife through paper
Leaves the spikes
To prick into consciousness
For the rest of this life
There is no mending;
The black blood has gushed out
Filtered from the red,
That bubbles into rebirth.

18   *Geometry of the Mind*

His eyes
Black
Will hypnotise
Force my mind
To bend a right-angle to his own.
The will
Will never submit
To this geometry
Black eyes
Upon my black fear
Can force a rape.

19   *The Consolation of Illusion*

The consolation of illusion
Love and light
To clean with over-exposure
The grimy patches
A fixative would do better the trick
To see
Black upon grey upon white
The cold knife edge
Saw amputating limb
The cut of day

20   *Will*

The will frittered out
Would not obey
Turned perverse
I tried to call it back
They tried to call it back
It ran screaming over the earth in all directions
The coal beneath the clumpy tree trunks
Turned black
Filamented into spider roots
We waited
A stone's throw
A flicker of wind
That scratched and teased the hush
In expectation
And swivelled
To the right key
Pleased to turn back.
Back into turning

21 *Between Before and After*

Falling short
Compromise
As the air filters into yellow and blue
From what was conceived
To what has grown to be
This instant
Flickering dust
And choice of words
Could be perfected
To a pearl
Static
There at the centre
All other objects dropped
Now
Frozen
Into a realisation of what has been lost
The curves and angles shudder
Between before and after
Swing into focus.

22   *The Hum of Silence*

Hot silence
Divides the air
Into good and evil
Listen to the hum of the world
Blink
Numbly.
Now if a curtain of moon
Would eclipse the sun
And turn the world into a black grimace
Where would we laugh
Which part of the cheek would grin,
Dissolved with the palsy
Of light
Blank gold of light
Releases the terror
Throw off daytime shapes
A kaleidoscope
To divert the heart from a love
That can never be released
Never swell into a burnt flood
Trapped inside the hum of silence
Of the revolving earth.

23 *Guilt*

Gilted leaves
That paint the sun
Over their web of spider-stem
The guilt I feel
For past misdeeds
That cannot be
In knotted pain
The crab that grew
When he told me
Of the guilt I own
This clod of earth
Twists into folds
Beneath the sun
The evening light
Goes down
Goes down
One day will roll away
Beyond
The edge of some world basket home
The retribution will begin
The guilt I own
The knotted crab
Will tell its gold.

24   *Combat*

If you could love the person
Whom you most dislike in all the world
Then you would have conquered fear
To kiss the repulsive lips
And smile with feeling warmth
Upon the face you loathe.
If you could spend one day and night
In the house which you most abhor
Then you would have conquered your fear.
But here is no victory possible,
Only an endless sidetrack along a devious maze
Away from the dragons that people
The kaleidoscope of your mind.

25   *Infatuation*

Every time I fall in love
Sharpness of sunlight, silhouette
And glow of silver reflection
The stab of passing you in the street
All faces grow alike, reflect the same expression
And I am thrown into the magnetic pool
Of one personality
Then slowly the surface thickens,
The sharpness turns to wool
And there is only a cold gust of wind
Until the next figure
Walks clearly onto the scene.

26   *Black and White Universe*

One man was there
I loved
Face black and white
I cannot forget
Stays there in the centre
A reminder of the one
We cling to
Which way to go
Right or left
Or to stay there in the middle like a rock
Everyone
Has one man there in the centre
Black and white
To clock in on time
And watch the whim
Of the black and white universe.

27 Cynic

She speaks glibly of intellectual despair
And I see blackness in her eyes, her hair
Her smile cracks her face in two
And my peace of mind is blown over
From its upturned wave
And crumbled into drops of disbelief
Her laugh is grating
A macabre mockery
And echoes in my mind at midnight
Turning my eyes and hair black
In the hanging gloom.

28 *Kite*

I can never know you completely
The more I know the more I want
Can never reach the peak
Looped kite flying against the cream sky
Can never reach so high, high
If I could fly
And loop the loop to cling to the top
I would pull you down
Crash into the seeking grass below
Wet from the rain
Splash into the mud
I can never know you at all
Not at all
Just the tug of the breeze that lifts
A flicker here and there
And then slithers away
Into stillness.

29 *Primary School*

On a windy morning in October
The first week at school
Two rows of children were lining up
Hopping up and down
Pale legs turned orange in the damp air
In the school playground
A girl named Mary
A boy called Graham
Strange to meet other people in the wind
Each with different features
Fitting together like the faces we crayoned
That morning in the long gone schoolroom.

30   *Adulthood*

Hideous jollity
Kipper on the table
And a smear of margarine
Loudspeaker turned up full blast
Into words and noise and words
Battering ram of information
To churn through the kitchen sink water
That flows from an open tap
Onto the square handle
Of an upturned yellow beaker
The three walls press inwards leading me
Through the open doorway
And crack open the front door
To squeak through the bulge of the narrow hall
White stinging sky
Clap-shock of rebirth
Into a non-plastic world of rainwater
Soft moisture in the air
And the angry grey December
Stretching endlessly
Towards the city.

31 *Three Witches*

When my anger broods and stirs
Within me, black bubble liquid in a cauldron
And the three witches grin and leer
Over me, yellow teeth rotting in mirth
Hatred sizzles my love for you into distrust
And fear turns ice cold white skin trembling
As I wait for your retreating figure
To return and smile
But it remains far distant
And jealousy burns into my stomach
With wild insistence
The black bubbles brood
And the night sky outside
Hangs like a slate
Flat against the glass of the window
Pain against pane
Until gradually the old love rolls over me like a wave
And all I see are your shining eyes
And outstretched hands.

32 *Shades*

I see you shadow-bound
Between the circle of life and death
Grasping at every moment
An extra person to acknowledge your existence
I see you at the leaf-time
Brown evening shadows against the wall
When you are beige
A biscuit figure
Grinning and seizing the faces there
With a smile and a nod of the head
I know that to be dead
Is to be remembered
Yet I cannot act as you would wish
Hand outstretched, giving to all
In the face of every attack from the shades of night
For to me the night has no shades
And I have no need of these people.

33 *Deserted*

So many things given
Mornings that sweep open the sky
To set me free
And fluorescent twilights
Navy pools of night
Even the still band of ice
Across midday
That freezes the clamour into peace
So many things given
Then why should I mind
That you will not give
One word
One shadow of your presence?

The blank space
Through which furniture and walls protrude
In your place
Screams endlessly
A nightmare;
A vacuum;
A desert
Of being deserted.
One whiny woman
Cannot bring back all those who have escaped
Slipped through the tracks
To sweep open the sky alone

And break the navy pools of night
In solitude to regain
The still band of ice
For which they crave.

So many things
God has given me
In every place there are signs of Him
Then why do I see
Only the empty spaces
And no freedom?

34 *Salt*

Sunday afternoon,
White as salt
I walked over the dregs of the building site
In slow motion
A woman nearby pale with a broken arm
Placed each foot two inches in front of the other
And groaned with effort, swallowing two aspirins
The concrete blocks on either side
Washed clean the past
In slow waves of walking
Our cold eyes stared
Grey pupils, molasses of concrete
And as she passed over the bridge
I recognised the swing of navy skirt
And saw again the young smile
And hand outstretched with chalk
In the classroom of the fourth form
Through the windows the June sunshine
Streamed onto the walls of the chemistry block outside
And I knew that the past had been wiped clean as a slate
As clean as bromide paper
Left in the sun too long
And bleached from over-exposure
White as salt.

35   *Before and After the Darkness*

Things are not so easy for you now, my love
There is much work to be done
Much darkness to be swept away
As I walk along the bleak street I see
A Christmas tree
Red balls of light on khaki branches
The only Christmas tree I could give you
Would be a heap of lollipops for your children
For the child that you once were
Before the darkness came upon you
Before you saw too deeply within
If I could help you along the way, my love
I would do so willingly
But there is too much work to be done
For one person or even two or three
Too much darkness to be swept away
Darkness and shadows
Equivocal and obscure.

36   *Future Nightmare*

I dreamt I had a tiny ear growing inside my ear
And stood in the brown rustlight in a field of wheat
Yellow and buff leaves flopping crisp
Yet unwholesome
The cardboard cracks torn down
Between the possible and the unearthly
I had become a painted cartoon
On a packet of shredded wheat
And lived in a future era
When all things could grow awry,
In the barley and the rye
Dinosaurs wriggling along the fields
With grey charcoal hippos
Hanging vertical in the painted air.

37   *Earthquake*

The girl sways her pregnant hips
As she plays on the guitar
Silver rings, flash of light, sparks in the fire grate.
Slither through the silver grid
She sings a losing song
The song of those who have wasted hours
Washing, knitting, furlongs of wool
Who have slipped through the tracks in boredom
And hours of friendship snapped in two
By a letter gone astray
Dropped in the sizzling heat
At the end of a long day
The losers of this world
Gather together their energy
And form rings around her guitar strings
But no rings on her stubby fingers
No colour on her scrubbed white face
Chin jutting out squarely beneath ashen hair
And eyes like long blue fish
That slither and smile
As the audience around her swells pregnant
With all the ticking hours of her life
That have never been channelled into
Certitudes or bonds
Who have fallen away, disappeared
For men who have slipped away

Through the tracks in boredom
And only appear from time to time
Silver cools in the earthquakes of her songs
But smoulder under the ground
Between the cracks.

38 *Not to See Him Again*

Not to see him again
Never the eyes crinkling
Lips twisted
Into a smile
Not to speak to him again
No more answers
To insoluble questions
No more clues to a magical formula
For living
Not to laugh with him again
No eyebrows raised
With new apologies
Communicating where further communion
Was prevented
Now we are joined by the black ligaments
Of memory
Blood beats around the sinews
And can never rest
Lives on forever
In the hearth-fires
Of a generous heart

39   *Whale*

Despair, the whale
Swallows up the whole man
And then spews him out
To taste the golden waters
Beneath the dazzled sky.

40 *Ants*

Ideas
Like ants
Multiply, swarm and flock together
I am careful
Which way I turn
So as not to crush
A few thousand.

41   *The Squatter*

Bare carpet peeling off
Soft fluff
And on the walls a picture
Of the Maharaji
Gaudy colour posters
And unswept dust.
The squatter's clothes in a bundle
In front of the paint-smeared bat window
Which dazzles the naked room
Like a scream
After childbirth.

42   *Housewarming*

They scrub the drawers
And sweep clean the carpet of dust
Three unopened cases and two bags of provisions
Gradually
The room unfolds its colours
Like a tulip bending over its reflection
Until petal and water kiss
In one bubble of colour.
Outside
The May streets
Sways with birds and trees
Welcoming them
To their new home.

43   *Rhythm*

Each day month week
We polish shoes shine
Feathers dusted
Oven scrubbed
Face washed
In the blood of diurnal rhythm
Breakfasted many times
Car restarting on the same journey
Alarm-clock shrieking
Trapped in the twenty-four-hour
Game of chance
Again
Again
And again.

44 *It Will Pass*

May
Peace   birds   trees   sway
Welcome
Window looks onto rooftops
Pale cloud sky
Two youths saunter
Towards each other

Always
The past is made concise
Tied down to daylight frame
While the present
Muddles though
Blurred-edged

Every time
I feel suicidal
I remember this:
'It will pass' –
It helps me

45   *Lunch*

Four girls
Sharing gossip
At lunchtime
Hair tossing aside
In different shades of brown
One strand over this forehead
Two strands over that
Stab a tomato and pull this man
To pieces
Spear a lettuce-leaf and murder that one
Now a laugh
One joke
Two jokes
Three smiles
Four empty plates.
Silence.

46 *Memories of a Solemn Childhood*

Crisp voice, newly ironed
Along with the frilly white blouse,
Skirt swinging, flick back the hair
And run down the hall on pattering shoes.
Carnation scent, a belt of leather studded with gems,
Staccato laugh, pinching the world
Into delicate shapes of comedy,
Like an expert *patisseur*,
To slice reality into thin strips,
More manageable.
Gravity annihilated
By microscopic analysis,
Probing the components. seeking out the absurd.
Occasionally
To sink into a chair and cry,
Shoulders heaving,
Memories of a solemn childhood.

47   *Beethoven*

You teach me how to plumb the depths of pain
In tuneful melancholy probing deep.
Then numb my thoughts to quietness and peace
Inducing an unexpected, timeless sleep.

Your melodies each plead with me to listen
To their twofold message splaying from one source.

In artful harmony, which once perfected
Leaves nothing unresolved by its polished force.

48 *Day and Night*

The day slips across the murmuring sea of life
Borne aloft on a single wave, precarious and about to totter.
Despite the floating seaweed and driftwood that hinders
       its course
It travels from shore to shore with unrelenting regularity.
Never stopping to pause and survey the scenery
Or to give way to an oncoming intruder.
When a ship rumbles near at great force
And continues its journey in submarine silence
Until it reaches the far side,
When it is again restored to the breathing air.
Night comes on the face of the sea
And time glows with phosphorescent brightness
Illuminating the nocturnal world of fishes
Into a glowing unity.

49 *Fire Song*

I hung upon the splintering beam of oak
That shouldered me and pricked with cutting lashes,
But held me high above the burning timber
That crackled as it crumpled into ashes.

The flames subsided soon and turned to cinders
I swept them up and burnt my little finger.
It smarted but then drifted into numbness
And soon I overcame my hasty anger.

50   *Time Frozen*

Time frozen into ice-drops
Clings quietly to the branches
Of the pear tree by my window.
A gust of wind impels it into motion,
Scattering it into a myriad of pearls
That fall to the ground and clink bitterly
Regretting their release from immobility.
Once static, now reluctantly individual,
They drift sadly in all directions
Longing for the winter of eternity to chill them
Into icy permanence once more.

51 *Time's Whispering Silence*

I hear time's whispering silence in my ears,
A toneless beat that never stops to linger.
Sometimes it overtakes my drifting life
And leaves me far behind in useless anger.

I take a running leap to overtake it,
But trip upon the hurdles of existence
And when I try to grab its furtive sleeve
It slips away from me with slip persistence.

52 *Crocodile*

I know a man
Who goes to church every Sunday
And works in Moorgate in a black bowler hat,
Quite an ordinary man,
Except that when he was a boy
He read of the African jungle gleaming wild and free
And lived between lessons in a towering date-tree
Half a mile high
And whistled eerie songs to the crocodiles,
That squelched and chattered in the churning mud
Of the Lualaba River,
And stamped angrily on the crawling red ants
That used to invade his unobtrusive hide-out.

And when he was sixty and a half, he retired
And in return received a splendid watch of solid gold
To tick away his senile years of leisure,
When he was supposed to prune the rose-heads
And drink amiable cups of tea with his quiet, pleasant wife,

But instead he went straight to the zoo
And took home a tiny tame crocodile
With horny skin and tender eyes and flashing teeth
He fed it on raw meat and milk and peppermints,
Which crocodiles are supposed to greatly relish
And at last he was thoroughly absorbed,
Hauling up plates of food and whistling eerie songs.
Even his wife didn't seem to mind
In spite of all the squelching and spilt water
For she was quiet and pleasant.

53 *Silver*

Why, when I look at silver,
Can I not see the compound colour
White, grey and black
But see only the shiny metal surface?
And why, when I look at you and you and you
Can I not see the compound colours
But only the fixed image?

54   *Fear of the Lone Self*

This park greenery
Overwhelms
Like a memory of nausea
Damp tufts of grass upon clod of earth
Tickle the feet
With fear of the lone self.
The ruthless clock of time
Throbs noiselessly
Beneath the fertile veneer
Of the earth.
Hours spent in the naked light
Of the midnight room
And the opened book
Palling
After isolation
Waiting for the sound of the foot
Upon the stairs
The squeak of the rat
Now
Amidst running children
And sleeping torsos
Impossible to shout
'I am alone!'
Alone beneath a body of skin
Waiting
For what can never come to pass.

55 *Tree and Leaf*

Books   dust
Woolly paper   at edges
Torn covers   brittle spines
People reading, reading
All over the world
Swallowing indigestible phrases
As well as the old familiar
Concepts
Dust falls to
Floor
Outside trees grow to wood
To paper   to books
Hieroglyphics of black and white
Feeding the brain
Which feeds the body
Which moves among dust and wood and paper
And books and trees, where
The birds whistle happily
Having read nothing but the signs
Of tree and leaf

Index of Poems

Index of First Lines

527

Falling short / Compromise / As the air	*Between Before and*	BAAD	483
Fear of motherhood. / A broken glass	*No Mother*	DOS	155
Five different faculties have we unknowing	*Eyes*	ISMH	416
Fixed / Upon a tulip / I saw / Blue tinged	*Tulip*	ISMH	448
Flames and torture-rack of a Tudor epic	*Stepping Outside*	ISMH	354
Fools / That grin and have faith	*Those Who Do Not*	ISMH	314
For four years we have worked in the	*Communication in*	ISMH	251
Force open these eyelids shuttered so	*Waking*	ISMH	237
Four girls / Sharing gossip / At lunchtime	*Lunch*	BAAD	509
Frost and fog through the windows	*View*	ISMH	332
Frozen fingernails turning yellow	*Blackbird*	DOS	106
Gilted leaves / That paint the sun	*Guilt*	BAAD	485
God / Spreads his / Warmth and peace	*Praise*	DOS	221
Grey slaps that peel down / To neat shapes	*Occupational Therapy*	ISMH	441
Hair aflame with the heat, / Eyes	*The Reading*	ISMH	258
Hatred dwells among people, / Like	*Verdure*	ISMH	317
He mocked her drawing, / Black criss-	*The Killing*	DOS	54
Heart cracked into jagged edges / Like	*Cracked Heart*	BAAD	479
Heat dissolves me, frees the barriers	*Heat*	DOS	122
Her head is cider-swollen to a bubble	*No Danger*	ISMH	345
Her voice hit the air with a subtle sweep	*The Singer*	DOS	121
Hidden in a telephone kiosk / On an	*Last Respects*	ISMH	351
Hideous jollity / Kipper on the table and	*Adulthood*	BAAD	492
High above the earth / Upon a tightrope	*Rope*	DOS	74
His anger murdered her with eagle eyes	*Bones*	ISMH	301
His eyes / Black / Will hypnotise	*Geometry of the M.*	BAAD	480
His moccasins spattered with green mud	*The Rendezvous*	DOS	44
His poised / Eyes, / Leaping fish	*Fishing*	ISMH	303
His writing is more real to him than life.	*To Write*	ISMH	383
Hot silence / Divides the air / Into good	*Hum of Silence*	BAAD	484
Hypocritical / With each change of	*Involvement*	ISMH	424
I accept this, the stifled past / I can endure	*Acquiescence*	ISMH	433
I am a child of the twentieth century	*Twentieth Century*	DOS	163
I am a puppet, / Jerking one and two and	*Puppet*	DOS	150
I am a shell / Catching echoes of the past	*Shell*	DOS	141
I am a turnip gone mouldy / And my top	*Corrupt*	DOS	177
I am an egg. / A black band in the middle	*Egg*	ISMH	389
I am frightened of the night / That suckers	*Frightened of the N.*	BAAD	472
I am one person/Sometimes the snowdrop	*Snowdrop*	ISMH	438
I am pale and white / Calm and quiet	*Chastity*	DOS	41
I can never know you completely	*Kite*	BAAD	490
I could tear you out of me,	*Chicken Bone*	DOS	67
I do not know / Whether I have the	*Surprise*	ISMH	355
I dreamt I had a tiny ear growing inside my	*Future Nightmare*	BAAD	499
I felt myself falling through a hole in the	*Return*	DOS	197
I have forgotten it, / The guilt which lay	*The Losing*	DOS	112
I have known you in another life	*Shadows*	ISMH	299
I have nothing, / Unless I have all	*Spur*	DOS	171

www.ingramcontent.com/pod-product-compliance
Lightning Source LLC
Chambersburg PA
CBHW021207090426

42740CB00006B/159